BE NOT AFRAID

By

James Ellis

To Fr. James Walsh, for your patience and guidance.

PREFACE

This book was written prior to my Baptism and Confirmation within the Catholic Church, secondarily as a way to document the internal struggle of an atheist to Christian convert. But primarily the book is written - hopefully - as help for those young men and women who have come to the end of their tether with regard to the modern world, and in moments of silence still yearn for something more. If this story helps but one person move closer to the Lord, then I shall consider it a success.

I must also acknowledge my debt to a handful of writers whose work has directly influenced and inspired this book, most notably C.S. Lewis, Edith Stein, Thomas Merton, Michel Serres, Maurice Nicoll and Emil Cioran. Secondly, this is a work of fiction, and where allusions to the supernatural are found they are solely imaginative, I do not seek to suppose neither what awaits us, nor *exactly* what stirs our internal discussions with God.

James Ellis, March 2022

I'm trying to imagine a spaceless world - and all I can find is the heart of a saint. – Emil Cioran, *Tears and Saints*

For by doing what God demands of us with total surrender of our innermost being, we cause the divine life to become our own inner life. Entering into ourselves, we find God in our own selves. – Edith Stein, *Finite and Eternal Being*

Per crucem ad lucem.

PART 1: THE BAKERY

It had been some time since reason had called for me to look upon that profoundest chaos; where nothing ever settled, and not even brackets screwed to the wall could discover rest. And yet, grievously, it was here where this young man found himself, unsure as to the length of his sentence, nor how he had enrolled, or to the cost of such deepness; in fact, he was quite unable to locate himself at all. For a time, this young man existed - or so he had recursively taught himself to believe - as simple clothing atop life, subsisting alongside material as something which only is, and not as a being with the potential for fullness.

In truth, that is, in speaking for reality, he found himself in a place quite transparent. I know, for I kept a keen watch of this young man for some time, a task which must be accepting of various wills. He entered where I had hoped for him to not, and yet still did. And so, 'twas my divine task to simply observe, waiting upon such hopeful moments where one is called to a divine duty.

~

Don't know how I got here, or how long I've been here, couldn't really tell you. Not the best job in the world - some dull retail store in the middle of nowhere - not the worst though, far from it...and there are plenty like me. No one ever comes here, no one visits, no one bothers us. Anyway, none of this matters; boring town, empty people, all just forgettable, pointless. Could do better things, but it'll do. All this achievement tripe...success, failure...needless; just need to forget. People used to say I could do better, that such a place wasn't for me, whatever any of that means. Others have interests, hobbies and the like, some acquire habits and vices, myself? Even an addiction or an illness would be a reprieve from this lethargic disquiet.

~

I drifted, I guess, you know? That's how they like to phrase it, and I suppose it makes sense. But what's wrong with drifting? I've seen people with roots, succumbing only to routine and boring lives; such value-laden lines adhere to the earth in a spindled panic, clawing at the dust in fear of ever letting go. Anyway, like most normal people I hadn't a clue, did what I was told; bits and pieces here and there, stayed in education until I had to pay for it or it was too much effort, occasional parties, having fun, ups 'n downs as they say. Mostly a blur now, snippets of various things I did a while ago, all out of order and confused. And then one day you end up in a place like this, a friend only to yourself, distrusting trust due to its definition alone. And it's like a sort of sentence, but in reality, you get used to a place like this after the first couple of days, understanding you're the kind of person who's meant *for* it. Some are privileged, 'get all the luck', as they say...you know the type. But most, they're like me and you, dragged and dragged. Been a while since I spent any time thinking about this place; there's no detail here, the arrival is lost to time; a caring amnesia. It's all beside the point, it's not like I'm here and could be elsewhere, I *am* here. There is one thought which is of no help here, and that is of difference.

~

I ask myself if it's worth the effort to describe such a job, such a place, and yet the reason escapes me as to why I have even bothered with this line of thought at all. It is...whatever it is. In fact, no, it isn't worth my time to describe it, but then, what *is worth* the time? Nothing I've yet to find. Caught in my own trap. If it's not worth it to explain this to you for the fact of its nothingness, then it's equally as pointless to *not* explain it to you. So it comes down to whether or not I can be bothered.

Such places, such jobs, such times, they developed organically with people like me and you in mind; the most persuasive nihil awaits the eventual hordes of indifferent apathists - but at that point, it hasn't a need to *persuade.* You and I shall *end up* in these vocations; they have a draw and pull which is itself inescapable, best to just lean into it. Did that a while back and time doesn't bother me anymore, it just *passes*; impossible to squander the seconds of your life if you never allowed them value in the first place.

So, yes, the job that I do...I am a baker, but truly that is a glorified name for someone who reheats some artificial mixture. It's thrown into the oven, a certain setting is clicked on, a while later you're left with a mass of dull, tasteless stuff. I pay no attention to the food. Has it ever been in *anyone's* job description to care? But it is this, day-after-day, a repetition so perfect it clouds each day with the next; work becomes, and has been for time immemorial, a drawn-out vacuity, empty space taking up empty time.

~

But I admit, as my mind is drawn from its preferable slumber, in this head full of perpetual fog, I ask myself how it was I got here - but no! Of more importance, what could it be which spurs on such thoughts? It needn't matter, home time soon enough, and then another day awaits. Tough to notice the transition between here and elsewhere; I can't say here is detachment from reality, for I cannot recall ever abiding by such groveling notions as partiality or...*fondness*, but one is pleasantly severed none the less; bombs could fall, cities crumble, the end times arrive, and here, here would be safe, it would remain, I just know it.

And as one is severed, I notice that we here are severed from all illusions, and all lies, and from all those who won't admit to what is within them; there is no reality to elude here, for we have a monopoly on it. I say 'we', but it truly is just myself and the boss down here, I speak of we as to include those who are here with me in absent idleness. Every thought of some or other *place*, this is tyranny, a deceit of self. It is to cheat oneself out of what is before one's very eyes in a vain attempt at allowing imagination to rule.

Here is where I am *to* be, meant to be, was always to be - and here I am, all in its right place. It is with such clarity that

I cease to bother, it is absolute for me that this is the case, and so I have no need to prove it to you, nor qualify anything at all, for I am not *asking* for anything; depression would denote the desire for happiness, and anxiety the lust for calm - but what if you have given all over to nothing, becoming an agent of pure-disinterest? I know my place in this world, it was decided, long ago, I - unlike some others - simply accept it; here I am to be, all else is existential-fraud.

~

Within such times, it is to one's benefit to become an aristocrat of apathy, entirely in flux, one who has ceased to care for any laying of roots. One needs to be able to move from all to all without question, else be left to the tyranny of values; to be knighted by the relative, an honor which is not even itself.

~

As should be known by now, this place isn't all that bad once you get used to it, sort of just disappears. But I assume you're wondering what it's like, how it looks and feels, there isn't much to tell...but a guide, I suppose.

At a guess this building could have been an old post office or something of the sort. Maybe an electrical store long since renovated, patched over and held together many times, still here though, trembling at its foundations, never able to collapse. Nothing fits right, the ovens jut out into the walkway, the uneven shelving always knocks your brow, steps shift, and the temperature brings a fever never shaken. As to see the oven monitors, a thick tape covers the only window which the heat once used as its escape; it's sweltering, and yet my limbs don't know warmth. Nothing stands out, it takes years before you begin to notice any differences between the decor, and even then, it's a strain which quickly dissipates. Everything merges into everything, and so, everything becomes nothing. My dramatic perspective aside, it's a bakery section below a generic chain-supermarket. That's it really, ignore all I've said. I rarely spend time upstairs, couldn't tell you the last time I was up there or had anything to do with them; I arrive by a side-door.

In fact, outside of the bakery, I couldn't tell you anything about the rest of this place, my work is here, and it keeps me busy enough. It doesn't bother me anyway, it takes a certain person to deal with customers, and I can't stand them. It's a fairly large room down here, however, I can't think of anything to measure it against. You lose your focus and attention, and the space appears to expand and contract. Me and the boss once joked about it expanding forever, that made him laugh more than I'd ever heard him laugh. As it's a basement, there are no windows, except for the one above the side-door I mentioned before, but as I have already said, that needs to be taped up, boss' orders, lest I mess up my work, but I don't mind. It's no matter anyway, everything I want is across from the door, I have no need to turn that way.

As for the rest of the place, your imagination is probably close to reality, most people know this place well enough already - it's pretty filthy, the brick is old and dry, and yet there is dampness to the air. There are two ovens, some cooling racks, and a huge work surface along the far side wall. I have never reached the end of it. My work takes place amidst old mortar, the endless whir of ovens, and a wet-heat which protrudes into your cells. That is about all I can grasp for now, for if you know of this places' minute details you would understand that it doesn't allow such limits; it's endless in all directions, each, as I have found, leading nowhere. And so, you keep your head down, and exist.

~

It doesn't matter what state it's in, no one comes down here, and as I think I already said, we don't get visitors. When I say we, I am speaking of myself and Ollneek, the boss. In fact, that I *can* mention, it slipped my mind before - I often forget he is here at all. Ollneek's office is to the left of the ovens, at the end of a corridor, I'm not sure how long. His office is to the right, and across the hall is a huge walk-in freezer, though I haven't had use of it for a while...which, thinking about it now, makes little sense. I don't know. Anyway, I imagine there is stuff in there from the beginning of time.

This reminds me, though I haven't thought of them for some time, there are other tunnels off from this other corridor, the one which leads to the boss' office. They tend to blend into your peripheral vision as you walk by, you can only *catch* them; much here is caught, as if trapped, within the cracks of basic connection. I think this place must have originally been built during a war, I intuit tunnels below spiraling in all directions. Ollneek knows I'm not too keen on talking about them, teases me about them, I think he'd love to see me down there, set me on my way, as he says. I haven't had the need to explore them as of yet, my job is here, and if such is without value, then I do not hold out for elsewhere.

I haven't recalled any of this in some time, but there was a young trainee down here a while back, to be taken under my wing. He arrived early, I recall, and by lunch Ollneek had teased him so much about those tunnels that this kid, very proud and quite young, ventured without hesitation. I think I told Ollneek at the end of the day that the kid hadn't returned, but Ollneek said simply to go home and not worry about it as it wasn't my concern, and so I did.

~

I may have to think upon home in a while as something there eludes me, but for now I think I need to clarify what I mean about this place, to...articulate it, that is. I am sure you are imagining the brick and the gloom, adding in spider webs and masses of dust, the detritus of a labyrinth. Physically, such corrosion is close to the truth, and yet it seems only to eternally decay and yet never change. It is not abject horror, and yet is not close to anything I can grasp; such extremities cannot exist here, for as springboards they allow contrast and thus a compass, here there is only disorientation; definition dissipates upon entry. It has been my home for some time, I don't know how long. As for what you might consider my real home, I go there often, but also cannot remember the last time I was there, nor even walked close-by.

But my place, really? It is here. My place is exactly this place. My childhood simply *was*, then the usual amount of booze, drugs and sex, a good amount; some 'education', blustered around for a while, and now I'm here. There's no need to kid myself, this was a foregone conclusion. I'm not complaining, all men lead such lives, and very few complain. No time for anything else anyway. I know this is me.

This place is for me, and I am for this place. The work here won't do itself.

~

Overhearing the young man's melancholic prelection, Ollneek - as he was then known - coyly arose from office, protruding hue into hallway and observing a posture bolstering his nature, he stood leant against oven, facing into the cold brick expanse; the young man's eyes to his work, Ollneek began again.

'Young boy, I can hear you squawking, with the wherewithal for talking down here, loud 'n proud, as they say - what of it and what say you youngster of a worker's breast?' - Ollneek had a way with language, a self-proclaimed master of oration; he could transform the most mundane of wants into a terminal requirement. In a moment of pause one time, he commented on his manner, and said that you need to try and control such a place as this, 'Lest the order descend into chaos, and we become like animals.' or something of the sort.

'Was just talking to myself as I work, Mr. Ollneek, sorry to disturb.'

'Not at all, not *at all* youngster!' As the Old Goat spoke, he stretched the final syllable of a sentence to a destination unintended. 'It has been quite a while, has it not, since me and you and you and me have had a chance for an ol', as they say, chinwag. So, indulge me indulge me, what was it you were muttering about, so, by the sounds of it, passionately? For, and do not let this concern you, but I must admit, I did listen in, just a little. I was sure it wouldn't bother you, and these walls are so indiscernibly thin that one hears it all.'

He collogued and wheedled, but ultimately, above all, waited with the patience of his opposite for a chance again to unreel his views.

'Oh I see, well I've been here so long I was simply thinking over my situation, I'll keep it down.'

'Not at all young'n, not *at all* young one. Do tell, do tell. What sort of situation are we talking about here, good? Bad? Exciting? ...an escapade?' I had known Ollneek long enough to know exactly when it was he was about to reel you in, especially if he began with sarcasm or irony, he loved to tease without foundation. 'Come, come, I shall be serious for you my ol' friend, 'olde chum', as they love to say-'

Ollneek let out a shrill hiss, a laugh void of humor.

'-*you* are a dear, dear worker, and yet foremost you are a friend, a comrade, a compatriot, and we are all together in this. You have a situation which I shall assume is a problem. If you cannot talk to me, your nearest and dearest, then who, exactly, could you talk to?' I have to give Ollneek his due, he knew you well, almost better than you knew yourself, and could make you feel comfortable in an instant. 'I have been down here *some time* now Ollneek, that is all I was thinking about-'

'Ah! I see, I see, I understand exactly the situation of the sort you are waxing about. The Grand Vision! You have quite the desire to be - and I mean this my friend not in a way which is cruel - but you wish to be...Mr. Great! Mr. Known! Mr. Something-More!'

Prancing on hoof of pitch black, Ollneek mimicked men of shadowed-allegiance; the noise of below split asunder, all cut off aside from suggestive whisper.

My back was to Ollneek, yet I sensed he was appropriating the prideful and the go-getters, revealing their pretence; in his mimicry Ollneek had the ability to reveal that the humble were loudest, and those who sought desires were most honest, and it could not be any other way. Despite the didactic nature of these comedic tirades, I must admit, it makes this place so much better. 'Are you not going to turn around and fix a glance at those oh-so-grand-men who wish for the greatness of their meekness to be adored! Indeed, you think me a cantankerous old fool, but you know as well as I, that all is not meant for all, there is naught which is infinite, and it's best to not try in vain for a hope which shall never be and already is not; imagine a life spent in a search which has no conclusion. Far better never to rise to such a search, and accept the reality before you, for it is all there is - and what's more, it truly is not bad. I haven't the foggiest where you got such an idea.'

'I was only taking stock Ollneek, nothing more.'

'The only stock you should be taking is from the freezer at the end of that there hall!'

He was quite the quick-witted old fool, I had to give him that.

Ollneek said all that he needed to say, paused for time, assessed the situation, and stared dead into the back of the young man's skull.

'Ollneek, I have been here...I do not know how long, truly, I haven't a clue, and that's fine...I'm not pondering anything in particular, just reminiscing of a strange form.' All this time my head had been in my work, but Ollneek's presence was drawing me away from *doing* anything; it seems like years since I have even seen him; admittedly he has had little reason to be around, I've just been getting on of my own accord. However, it would be good to see how he is doing.

The young man spun slowly on heel; dropping momentary tasks such as to look upon Ollneek.

Alas, Ollneek's out of sight, somewhere at the end of the corridor, just beside his office, nothing to discern; something there I can't quite make out, perhaps he has returned to his office entirely; he usually likes to tell me what to do from his position of comfort - I seem to be able to hear his voice anywhere and everywhere.

'Well, I guess the thing is Ollneek-'

'Oh my dearest young boy, there is nothing and there is also no-thing, trust me. There never has been. Plenty have passed my way in the elusive search of some such supposed *thing*; they all had - and still have, for I *assume* they are still searching - oh-so-many things which they sought after in some illusory hope of conclusion. They shared the common thread which pertains to a magnanimous full-stop! Heed my advice young'n, for such searches are fruitless; the only harvest one can hope for is that which is immediately before them. In such a way, in this practical act of revealing, you have it all, a secure job, good friends, a good home, and productive work in a great company; try not to seek the invisible privilege of those who don't respect *this* world; the only real revelation is the one which draws back the curtain into nothingness itself, and from there, well, one can *become* anything. Can you imagine being king of such a domain? What an honor that would be, the mass...the mass of material before us all...anyway, I digress young one, but you are thinking past and beyond all limits, and they are limits which never were. Do not sulk on such facts that there is no other, no 'something else', for you now - thanks in part to my wisdom - find *yourself* within the elusive few who are willing to accept, and to admit to such truths, and that in itself shall be your liberation. Who needs something *more* to exist for, when you can accept the bare fact that existence is only ever lived for oneself?'

'I was just thinking-'

'Oh my young boy, I do understand such thoughts, trust me, I do. Such questions have been around as long as I have, and let me tell you, that is quite some time! But as I have said, there is no *thing* out there. I know what it is you are after, they, out there, all usually call it *more,* as I have already said. 'There must be something more...' they say, as they stare point blank into all there is, ignoring all its intricacies and complexities; before them all, the world, and yet they place their bets on something...more, 'tis all folly! I'm not speaking for you here, I'm speaking *of* you, dear friend. And even if I *was* to ask what is so bad about everything down here - as I assume you are referring to this grand bakery of ours - I know full well you would not be able to give a satisfactory answer. It's a simple job, rewarding, great company...great boss, and you know where you stand. Anyway, enough of such nonsense, I have heard these repetitions a thousand times before from many others like yourself, and I am certain this is the place for you. But I won't hold any of this against you, I know how alluring such 'other things' may seem, but I've yet to meet someone who could actually produce such an 'other thing', someone who could produce for me this something *more*, but as of yet, in all my years, not one has been able to show me such.'

I hadn't even time to reply before Ollneek was gone, leaving an answer set in the brick before me. Never knew what to make of him, up and down, all over the place. He never spoke of his past. But yet, he did keep an eye on me, making sense of things for me. Without his guidance, I sense a desert of the mind; Ollneek tells me very few are strong enough for such places.

~

Most days however, I must admit, I do very little of note. Sometimes I recall moving nothing at all. Often my eyes are looking for the time almost all of the day, spine reclining against the brickwork, the minute hand lost, but still my only comrade against this monotony.

But what does it matter if anything is done? To *do* implies a purpose, a purpose of which there is none - this loop defies me. Ollneek once said to me 'People without cares, no hope at all, doesn't matter anymore...what difference.' I hadn't and still haven't any idea what he was on about, either way I couldn't care less.

~

And so I got my head back down to work. For some time I mulled over what Ollneek had said, admittance to my error was easy, full-acceptance was not. And yet still, who was I to want for more, or wish for change; to ask for me to not be me, or for where I am to not be where it is. My place is my place, everyone has their place in this world, and for most it was never going to be what they wished for, hoped for. The idea of some*thing* is itself silly, dangerous even; the general inertia of existence is a great tyranny for precisely this reason, and its inherent stasis promises alterations which will never come.

~

I now remember arriving here; it's taken much time to dig up that old memory. I was around the age of 15, or so. No anchor, no feet to speak of on this trip. Ollneek wasn't the same back then - I don't remember why he approached me, or even if I approached him, though I think it may have been mutual - I can't truly recall. I remember that at first the bakery was suffocating - much like it has become in recent weeks - but back then, I got used to it very quickly, those feelings faded, and have only returned in recent times. This kind of place is only bad for the first few days, then you realize you're the kind of person who belongs in such an abattoir of being, or at least, such thoughts comfort the gradual descent. All other vocations had cast me out, little luck elsewhere, I just could not be bothered with all else, and so Ollneek offered me a job on the spot. The first shifts were really easy, liberating, even. Ollneek guided me, as if by hand, for a long time, until one day...I just got it, it all made sense. And with that, I no longer saw much of him. I mean, he had no worries, he knew I was more than capable of working for myself, it's only recently I've lost the passion for the job, maybe that's why I'm seeing more of him, he knows I need a refresher.

~

I have some memories of times before the bakery, I think. Times when I can recall what I assume to be named fun. Nights out, the frolic from house, to friends, to pub, a teleology of women and beer - oh what nights.

To recall the late night sessions, a haze of a sordid takeaway in the early hours. Awaking to a head weighed down by pain of regret and imbalance; nights of flesh followed by mornings of pure absence.

Never could correlate the guilt and loathing with any discernible source of displeasure, and yet such memories still sit rotten. Night after night of dull repetition. From the bellows of the bakery my memory attempts to solicit happiness from cliché reflections of debauchery, if there was little joy in the moment, of what use is such reflection for my current despair. And yet I *was* having fun, I must have been; and yet the heart admits, and the cost swells as a deep hue of sickness inside me. The senses given over to nonsense abused by the popular current of the day. All my memories are now an exercise only in attempting to forget, an erasure of a time given over to the bakery's foreign language. The modern act of 'losing oneself' is precisely that, an attempted suspension of existence, a terminal amnesia whereby one ceases to even remember that they are present; how many do we hear proclaim such nights must have been wondrous for they cannot even remember them, one can only assume that to be happy is to forget.

In truth, I cannot discern in memory between the good times and the times I wished were so, unable to crack a mere grin, I let my imagination take over - it seems, however, even that has grown weary. All that remains is a looped release of tension, a repeated predictable catharsis which, once looked upon in its false-grandeur, is only absurdity itself. Quite the fate. And so I decided simply to not think on such nights anymore, I admit to this past and these decaying memories, but I won't accept their absolute authority, even if what is left is but an expanse. I shall decide for myself, despite all contrary information protruding from heart and head that these memories are good, and so, now they are.

~

'I see and sense you got in rather late this morning, young'n?'

The young man could not remember when he 'got in'.

'Oh. Yeah. My bad, late one.'

'Well, spill, spill! I can tell you'd like to let me in on something rather pungent...'

'Was one of *those* nights.'

'Ah, a female...a female.'

'...a woman, yeah.'

'Whatever, whatever, divulge, divulge.'

'You already know how it is. Get chatting, few drinks, then you're at hers-'

'*That* easy these days? Well, yes, now I come to think of it, I guess it is.'

'Seems to be easy, yes. For both, though, not just men; the whole thing is a free-for-all, honestly.'

'I was going to...willing to, offer you some advice, but it's clear that you're not one who needs it.'

'...not like you to waste advice.'

'No, you're quite right, a little bolstering is always necessary, you could say. It is advice towards the goal of all goals then! Your little late night achievement. Such an explorer...'

'Not always so successful, as you know.'

'At least you are smart enough to see it though young boy, the reality of such things...yes, women! The fruit, the fruit! *The* prize, yes, quite.'

'How so? - I'm sure you have something prepared.'

'Don't feel you'll ever know me all that well, no such preparations here. However, as you say, best not to waste the springboard you've so kindly allowed me. Property, fancy clothing, charisma, flair, abs 'n muscles, even money, all surely and certainly great aspirations, but they all aspire to one thing, the aspiration to attract those 'women'.'

'That's certainly a theory, yes.'

'No theory young'n, not a man alive who'd bother with basic self-maintenance if not for the thought of ending the night in some stranger's abode. However, all this courting, all this patience...it is anathema to reality! There isn't a single woman who's passed my way who'd respect humble or meek men - 'What do women want?' modern men ask, what women want is a man who couldn't care less about what a woman wants, and to take only what it is he wants-'

'-which is, what exactly?'

'Well, it isn't *women* that men want exactly, is it? You didn't chat-up that young lass last night with thoughts for the future, thought for children or thought of wedding bells. You did so - if you are to admit - in the hope of entering into that state of eternal animality which is at the tip of all man's actions! All agency of man has a singular teleology, it culminates in that which makes one *blush* to mention.'

'Ollneek, I-'

'Do not stop me mid-thought, the pace and proof may never return. But, truly, think about it, if such a possibility was absolutely crossed-out, would you have bothered at all? No. So proof is in the pudding, as they say. Such acts rule the minds of all, the top priority of young ones especially. And for those who cannot indulge in this terminal pleasure, we all can see, as clear as day, that they move swiftly onto the next closest indulgence of the senses, that is to say dear boy, they get rather plump. For there is no greater meaning to *all this* than that pursuit of all pursuits...*feeling' good.* You look offended, but I only describe what *you* have told me, I merely show you who you are, and not what everyone else pretends to be. Without the possibility of pleasure, or feeling' good at the end of all things, surely the world would crumble in an instant. I doubt even that man and woman would have ever spoken to one another if not for that most crucial of things hovering below all communication. I wager you cannot even remember this young girl's name...'

Nonplussed, he could not.

'...see, priority, above all identity, affection and so-called love, the ability to lust. What say you? Have I not called you out? And not just you, but all the males I have ever met and spent some time with, lust before love; lust as that which makes one believe in love at all I say! And what admirable honesty to admit that the point of all is self and not other. Let us be honest, if not for the selfish desires of the helmsman, many a maiden would be lonely; marriages and relationships, mere securities to lock-in the continual self-justification of lust. And babies you say, accidents from pleasure - without such pleasure the world would decrease a trillion-fold!'

To my surprise, thinking back upon night after night, a flurry of random outings in memory, the names escape me, intermingling into a homogeneous recollection of vague sensuality, a light rot. Despite my efforts, I could not square reality with thought, reason with life; what was good in this did itself not feel...right; low and behold, lies of self towards that which self enacted. What I had told myself was right and normal, was at best absurd, at worst a darkness; the redirection of all efforts towards the most minor of pleasures and escapes, could there be more?

~

'Alas, young'n, at least *you* admit it has always been pleasure over product, for I am certain you took such measures?'

The young man remained silent.

'Of course you did. Rhetorically speaking, why *wouldn't* you, I have yet to find a reasonable answer to this query relating to the incessant continuation of all things?'

'To have children, surely that's the reason.'

'Yes, people keep *having* children, yes, yes. That is evident, for I keep meeting more such as yourself who need my help. But I am asking as to *why* they have them at all?'

'Ollneek, I'm sure your pre-prepared answer is fine, but I am tir-'

'Fine, fine, I shall lower my voice, you can keep on with your work as I talk. For this is one I am quite passionate about, as you may know. I know you won't mind if I talk and justify. You refer to a family, yes? Held together by that thing...love, nonsense, but it needn't matter here. If we have already understood the meaning to be pleasure, and pleasure to be the meaning of all things, then why would one consciously produce such whining, wheezing and wasteful brats? Am I wrong, or are they all liars? I think it's clear what the answer is. To give up security, freedom and passion for what? Sniveling and sponging, ludicrous! All children arise from a passion which missed its mark, a pleasure spoiled forever-more. And what perfect misery, what punishment for the betrayal of sensuality, a version of self mirrored before you for the rest of days; for your remaining years you must come face to face with your own flaws and failures in minutiae - and you are to argue the majority do this willingly.'

'Possibly something you're missing?'

'Ridiculous! Get back to work, I thought you were too tired.'

~

Weeks are passing by, I think. I work and work, I cannot recall any of what I have supposedly done. There were movements and actions - there must have been - but they amounted to nothing; despite ageing, I haven't built a thing. I have found that the term *life* is contrary to its verb-form *lived*, it's simply something to be endured.

~

All this work, of which I can remember none, as I have already said, is merely interesting in the manner in which it can merely fill up time. Some days, more often than not, I try not even to fill the time, I seek only to watch it pass me by; the great malaise of the silent clock. I *spend* my time thinking of when and where I was not. What use is memory if everything you can possibly think upon is always worse upon recollection, the brightness of the past searing into the shadow of the present; that gradient continues evermore, the future is black, a void. The work here comes prior to existence itself, if it was to cease I would be only some pounds of flesh taking up space. And yet the work, it doesn't exist, and we all know it.

~

Not once can I recall seeing a clock down here, wouldn't matter, that form of time is for those who seek, at any point whatsoever, to *do* something. It's for those with an end, a drive, a purpose - what's an hour to those unable to discern between winter and spring? Makes one wonder what a day is down here; my shift, when will it end?...and yet I have become so despondent, that I no longer even approach this as a question, just a torment.

This in mind, I have been thinking about the last time I went home. It's something which exists only in the faintest of memories, in outlined conception alone, an abstraction useful as a signifier in conversation. Often I feel the need to turn to the door, even just to see if it is still there, but this action never gets past preparation. I am held back by an oath to nihilistic-paralysis, fealty to the truth of nothing, where even bending a knee doesn't matter; I'll return to my work. And so, when I try to *think* of returning home, that is all I can really do. The reference and motivation are reduced to mere matter, dissipating as they collide with the atmosphere. Perhaps there is something there.

Paradoxically, for now, time has forgotten me.

~

The ever-stretched today has been an abject failure. A catastrophe of sense, with every step falling out from beneath each foot, all possibility of communication vanquished to the realm of absurdity. I sought to focus on my work, and yet even the handles of these cool ovens betray me, transparent to the touch, all bakes itself, and I am left without even agency as an ally. The bakery won't even afford me the morsel which is adheration.

~

'Young boy, whatever is such a grave matter, you seem to be, as they say, all over the place?'

'Mr. Ollneek...hello. Nothing the bother, too big of a thing-'

'Nothing too big for me to dispel young'n, nothing I tell you!'

'We spoke before about me being down here, and the, as you put it, elusive 'more' we all yearn for-'

"*We* all yearn for?', you mean *they* all yearn for. You, young boy, are of better stock indeed.'

'Sure. If what you say is the case, which I believe it to be, then what of purpose, meaning...direction? What are these for you?'

'Of course, it is, as they say, only a matter of time before this question arises; from the depths of all that is human comes the age old quandary of *me, me, me.* That is but a hint, but allow us to begin, although I am sure we have spoken of this a few times before my boy. Not the bother, after all, it is *the* question...*the* question, and yet you ask specifically of mine...well...I guess I'd best indulge you, hadn't I? But surely you must think, what could one's purpose be without others in the world to relate to? Could there be such a thing as purpose in a world of one alone? For my purpose, in a word, is emancipation...even...liberation! And without others, of what worth are these? In fact, they cease to exist. See now, I have run this place, as they say, since forever, since it has *been.* Many like yourself wander through, many go on and do things of great interest, others are more simpleminded, and...get lost, go elsewhere and do that which not a single man's sight notices. Needless to say young'n, all who come my way certainly take my lessons with them, not one has left without a piece of this place being silently lodged within their being. In this way, they can return here as they please, do you see, do you understand? As I said before, and shall say again until time dies a death, you are here because you are here, and you are here because you are *you*. But why would I, a mere bakery director, love my job oh-so-much? For it allows me to set up those that come through here, lost and then found, for a future in the world. Without need for recourse to further unnecessary lessons, people come and leave not as something new-'

Ollneek grew, and soared to the perimeter of all visible to the young man.

'-but as that which they *always were*. Ceased, gone and dispelled is this contemporary belief in newness and change, and long planted is a seed of my own mutation...no! A seed of my own creation!'

'I'm sorry Mr. Ollneek, but the question still stands, what of purpose? I don't feel you have truly answered me.'

'Yes, yes, no rush, no rush. For we have all night, and as I am sure you have noticed, here they are eternal. But yes, yes, ok, ok, let me answer this silly quandary for you, as they say, once and for all. Purpose, meaning, authenticity...the sincere, the honest et al, such things are all the young and old alike harp on about. Despite the supposed individuality of such pursuits, it is the masses en masse who squawk about purpose all the day long; the great collective which proclaims their separate autonomous meanings - what grand irony! And why do we think this is? Of course because they are nonsense, and those who proclaim them are nonsensical; empty words which wither away, and ultimately, were never to be found in the first place. The wise are not purposeful, or authentic, they are cunning and tactile - My purpose! To make you wise before your time, allow you the treasures of age without the droop of skin; what is experience if it doesn't allow for the acceleration of time? Meaning, purpose, the equation is - and always has been - simple, but you desire to believe that complexity equals coherence! And yet a subtle simplicity is all one needs...meaning is found where we create it! For all is relative, what is for one, may not be for you, and this applies to the entirety of man and all that is. Happiness is the purest plastic, no adherence, no striving, no *against*, no reaction, no struggle; friction drifting into nothingness, as one saunters between everything-as-nothing; one minute meaning, the next but a trifle! One second linearity, the next pure dissipation! Oh the beauty young'n of a purpose drawn from void, the flexible dominion of a thousand-thousand desires. And with this comes what, comes what? Yes, yes! Acceptance of self, such a state allows all and all to flow! My purpose is thus your purpose!

The young man attempted to speak, but Ollneek, dominating all sense, continued.

'-to what *end* though? Yes, yes, I know you are to ask! See, that too is inherent within all value, of what end is all that is done here in this world? Where are our actions to lead us? Which leads us to the question of why-oh-why we act *at all?* What is there, therefore, for us to act *for?* And what is it *to* strive if there is zero to strive *for?'*

Caught in the absurdity of Ollneek's prose and poise, the young man was stuck in a place without answer, groomed to ponder questions of no merit, any answer was further fuel for the fire of alienation.

I was stuck for thought, all answers eluded me.

'Young boy, you struggle, I see it. No worry, no worry, this is the case with all the young...and most of the old too! As if these questions you ask are of difficult answers, if such were the case would they not already be answered due to the plethora of historical human straining in relation to them. But no, such seemingly difficult questions have only not been answered because the answer is not simply *under* your nose, but quite literally *is* your nose; it is not a question of seeing what is *before* you, but seeing only yourself. The key is clear and many avoid it for fear of its obvious nature, but first I must ask...in whose name do *you* act? For whom? What is your goal?'

'...I simply don't know Mr. Ollneek; I am worried my answer will not be what you are looking for-'

'Boy, you lie and lie to *yourself*, answer is clear, no need to *look* for an answer at all!'

'Are you saying there is no meaning at all to my actions?'

'Senseless! An escape I say! But oddly...close. The question is simple, for *whom* do *you* act my boy?'

'...myself?'

'And here I was...worrying...worrying, and for no reason at all it seems. Finally young'n, I am so so proud. A pride of itself one could say.'

'A cliché though?'

'Oh...yes, yes, most definitely. But such clichés exist for a reason. For they are common, and there is none more common than that of which you speak.'

'Selfishness?'

'Why do you sound so *put-out?* You stand here so deflated...'

'Is it not generally understood to be a bad thing to be selfish or self-centered?'

'I did not know you were a general-man...*generally,* he says. And here I was thinking you *wanted* something more, or is that gone too, now?'

'I thou-'

'Check yourself as you speak! Listen to the words of your own voice, 'generally speaking', you say, as you denounce selfishness along with the herd; but why the collective denouncement from those who still practice that which they say they so hate? Because they want to feel better about themselves! Itself a selfish act no less! What is more selfish than he who slanders solipsism whilst continuing to frolic in its fruits!'

Ollneek filled the halls, the bakery itself, with a listless hue, cascading over the young man's shoulders.

"It is bad to be selfish' they proclaim, machines listening to the voice of their own unachieved false virtue; to desire for one's own is wrong, they state...and on and on, hopeless self-flagellation of self...all the while they suppress the yearnings of all sense! But why? Why is it so wrong to want for oneself alone? To be enamored by that which by rights should come upon one? For if there is *one* certainty of one's life it is in fact...*one*. That is, it is of I! To enjoy a desire, of course this is for one; to go up the career ladder, this is for you, we, I! - But yes, yes, those elusive acts of charity I hear you proclaim, what of them! It is obvious to those whose heads are not surrounded by sand, that one drops a coin in the beggar's pot to appease their own self! Driving Grandma to dinner, not out of...love, but out of a quiet hope for inheritance! In short, all that is done for others is truly done for self. Best you admit this dear boy, if only to be but a step ahead of the dullards and liars...'

'And if you are right, to what end?'

'End? There is no end! There's never been an end. The only ends ever created were those to pacify the anxious and meek; ends are implicitly for the weak of present. My boy, you don't need an end, what is it you wish to end? The acceptance of humanity's selfishness is itself the eradication of all ends. Even means don't matter. For what are means, ends, causes or effects if they are of no satisfaction to their user? They are nothing!'

'Satisfaction?'

'Oh boy, my boy, come on now...you must admit to what I proclaim?'

'Pleasure?'

'That's not *all* though, is it?'

'Well, pleasure, entertainment, feeling good-'

'Good, yes, yes, good!'

'...joy?'

'Let us stick with the first - the best of your life, come now, admit.'

'Possibly meals, drinking...sex, are you on about that kind of thing?'

"That kind of thing' the young boy says, as if there is any other. That which feels good, if not great, yes? What else to seek but this?'

'...there are of course other things.'

'Oh! Are there?'

'Marriage, children, a home? Not for me, but some oth-'

'Marriage! An archaic mess, a trifle, an excuse to party! A means to control. Children too can be stopped; sex allowed its true place, free from constraint of brat. And a home, this you have already!'

'Don't you feel that you are overlooking meaning and value, the larger things? Even if they are not for one, they may be for others?'

'Boy! I have explained before, time and time eternal. I have been around longer than all imagination. Many pass through this store, I have said this, I have seen divorce atop divorce, despair atop despair; these things you mention, mere aesthetics to hide such states of man! The cure I tell, the cure I say...vitality! The youthfulness of youth, frivolity, pleasure 'n leisure, these are the ends of all things; reason falls apart at the moment of sensuality; the memory forgets all bonds in the present of the senses, and so of what worth are these gratuitous customs of which you speak...'

'And what of love, then?'

'Love! Love! What utter folly! A grouping of two who sought the security of their personal, individual pleasure within the bureaucratic process of paperwork. There is no more to love than this, no above of love, men are simply animals attempting to avoid admittance of their base desires...no more!'

'And this is the end to all things, is it? Selfish desire?'

'What more have you ever sought? What more have you ever had need for...do tell!'

'I don't know. But perhaps I don't know because I've never experienced it, never...allowed it. Never opened myself to it, whatever it may be.'

'Allowed? Opened! This is sounding mightily like...hope, or that dear old fad of optimism; one wishes to *feel good* about themselves, do they? Easy to be led astray in the name of something you can neither see nor hear, why not stick with what you know? With what you can sense? There is pain and there is pleasure, these are the facts of life and reality, and it goes without saying that all are drawn to one and seek to avoid the other. For guidance in life, what can be of more use than these impenetrable facts, these two pillars of all purposeful direction?'

'Been a while since we've talked like this Ollneek, at such length. Maybe I can't find myself in agreement with you here. None of this makes sense, even the disagreement.'

The brick of the bakery bowed to master and tensed in time. For but a split moment, all illusion of faux-harmony cracked. Ollneek soared close to the young man, his voice a fragment between each instant.

'Well, what is it, spit it out boy! Let's see what ludicrous *hopes* you hold!'

'You spoke of being...led astray-'

'-yes, yes!'

'-By some-*thing* I can't see or hear, nor even sense in any usual way.-'

Before Ollneek could interject, the young man continued.

'But as far back as I can recall I have been led by only the most minor of whims, led by nothing, really; one day this, the next that, no correlation, no real path to follow. Led by an abyss I'm unable to grasp and yet has become my master. And where is it I am being led? My destination, seemingly final, is here, this strange elongated tomb, a bakery forgotten and lost; no thought for the outside world, just the two of us, non-existent and hemmed in. This other...thing, however, the one which is the cause of such discussions, and which you herald as distraction...despite its absence, I feel as if it is not real, but is that which allows anything to even *be* real in the first place; the logic of life itself; the foundation of all footing; a grammar which one may title...Grace. Of all the strangeness of this life Ollneek, perhaps I need to admit, or question why all the pleasure and leisure you speak of, all that which is apparently sought after as default by all - sex, drugs, drink, whatever... - all *that,* what are its promises, what has it promised all its users, myself included? I think I can tell you, for I have been such a user myself for as far back as memory allows. It promises freedom and makes slaves, promises happiness and brings misery, promises clarity and lends fog. And yet, worst of all, it promises individuality and hands out an equal portion of sordid conformity. I've yet to meet anyone of *this* world who is content, who isn't rushing around. All these people you speak of who declare hedonistic freedom as the greatest of all goals, I believe they proclaim their path the loudest as to drown out the sound of their emaciated hearts. Lost...lost I say. As am I! And so I grasp to this elusive something not as an escape, but in retreat; not as a diversion, but as the original destination, the only rest ever possible. And...I hope others feel the same.'

'Speak just for yourself boy! Most accept what is good and don't question such fruits like you!'

'What is the only world I have ever had? This one. The one passively afforded me, the one of whim and void. I've savored the best of this place, reveled in the juices of the fruits of which you speak, and for what? Today man is set to live a life more abundant than most kings of old, and where does he find himself at day's end? In a ditch of his own creation! I can *do* what *I* want, we can all do as *we* please, and it has led us only to a place where we can no longer truly act, nor even understand what it is we truly want.'

Ollneek, reduced to stasis in lowered temperature, made an attempt at sourcing an ultimate possession, the receiver was already down.

'...no answer from this atmosphere, nor from yourself, for I see it now, you don't speak the same language which has blossomed deep in my heart; even if it is but a single cell of Spring, that, I know, will be enough. And no, Ollneek, I haven't a clue where to go, or what to ask, nor whom to seek; I am asking for nothing, only waiting in an internal silence for the beginning of an answer, trusting that in such quiet mercy may be sown.'

'...you *poor* boy. You I pity. Sincerely, I do. Listen to yourself, looking for hope and meaning in something which simply is not here. You cannot even speak of it and yet find yourself relying on it. Folly, folly. Come back to reality.'

'This bakery, this 'reality', this...repetition, what does it have to offer me which I have yet to taste? I cannot accept that contentment can be found in getting even more lost. For if all you can offer me is what I have long since had, then I must refuse, lest I enter into another loop of this estranged distress.'

'What is this maze you speak of? The world is no labyrinth. There's nothing to get lost from, no elusive home. Anyway, enough! Get back to your work.'

'What work?'

'Well, we shall speak later, take some time for yourself for now. Take a break, do what you need. You'll come round.'

~

I must say, some time has passed since I thought about *this* situation, my situation... I couldn't tell you how much - maybe decades. But this tightness of being...this place. I must admit to something, it arrives from a place of in-articulation, and as it journeys to my lips it falters, breathing only inwards a warm internal sigh. It is not the acts which sit not-right, but the foundation itself, all is for naught and yet continues, pure absurdity. My life thus far has been inconsistencies kept quiet and contradictions getting along, for how long can such a knot of nonsense abide with itself before it collapses? Such a knot, I assume, is where one must begin.

Above the entrance door is a small window, I have mentioned it before, I think. It is covered in a thick black electrical tape. Nowadays the tape has begun to peel away, beads of light protrude over my shoulders. Once upon a time I used to patch it up, push the old tape back to where it was - but for now, what use, it seems to fall away of its own accord and so I just allow it to enter. All here seems to develop itself as for naught, for nothing - and so for rules grand and regulations small, why spare even a thought? There isn't a possibility for direction here, this I have taken some time to learn, and so now, I Am open to whatever may come. For I can't remember the last time I went home, nor arrived. My feet are caught in the flux of this basement, my movement bends to its whims; even now, in this moment of clarity, I sense its draw. I seek not passions! But I know not what else there can be; such words as belief and potential fall flat as they are announced, I wish for One who could teach me what they are to mean...

~

I just cannot remember anything. I must have gotten here somehow, this is silly.

I don't do anything, I expect to see Ollneek never again, and yet he appears. There are ovens, packages, and yet I seem never to use them. I can tell you in no detail what I do, and yet I do it. My time is simply *spent*. It is that I am both here and not here, in a place of fluxing-stasis, the work does itself and yet I help, I am very lost. Possibly, I do not know.

Who am I to utter such nonsense. People do things they don't enjoy, that is most lives. Ignore my moronic theatrics, Ollneek has warned me before of such whining.

~

The walls today are ever the same as before, no change in temperament, everything is as it has always been, and is yet trying hard to appear different. I find myself at the limit of repetition, the remainder of my life unspooling as a snake bored of eating its own tail, ignorant of what it is even doing; from here it is clear that it would take only a single sincere action to cascade a future of a thousand torments; possibilities closed by pushing on a pull door. A single seed of clarity can no longer be ignored, the deeply positive experiential fright of childhood, and the pure-nostalgia of a light not-yet known, but *felt*.

~

'Young boy, I can hear you chattering to yourself once again, what is bothering you?'

'Ollneek, if I am honest with you, I'm not entirely sure what it is I *do* here, what I get from it. I'm lost, I guess. Yes, I'm lost.'

'Why didn't you tell me sooner, I am always here when you need me, you know. But there is an idea here you unknowingly speak of. For when you speak of 'being lost', you once again assume there is some final place *to be*, or to head towards, and you must ask yourself, how can you be lost if there is no such thing as a maze of this manner? Young boy, we have spoken of this, but I repeat, no one and no-thing is seeking to find you, and so how can you be lost? And even if you are lost - as you say you are - then here seems a great place to be lost within, all you need, many delights, many treasures and pleasures... We spoke of this 'more' before, and I see now this all ties up - You believe you are lost, and that in 'finding your feet', as they say, you shall be found, and will perhaps find that elusive 'more' you have deluded yourself into believing in. I would advise you to stop being so critical of yourself, don't introspect so much, or feel you owe the world; you've no need to be found in this sense you have created, because you are perfectly fine as you are now. There is no need for newness, especially considering such a thing doesn't exist.'

'This is the thing Ollneek, even if that is all true, then what I am truly asking for in life, is not *more*, but less. I feel it must be simpler than all this, or at least could be. This elusive 'more', isn't complex, but overwhelming uncomplicated."

'You are speaking of very dangerous things, truly. What you speak of, *try* to speak of, *believe* in, simply does not exist. Hence the need for belief. These are not questions you can get inside of, because these questions are without answers. You say you are lost, and I say not so, and still you cling to some-or-other delusion you have created in the hope of...what, exactly? And see now look at what you've brought onto yourself, such questioning begets misery and insecurity, all was fine before, and you open some box and suddenly...chaos! I'd advise you not to talk like this down here, you know I'm not fond of rules, but this questioning mind of yours, it is not good for me or you.'

'Ollneek, I am sorry, but I cannot accept this.'

'Boy, what you mean you cannot accept?'

'Ollneek, I have heard all this before, all my previous years within recollection are a broken record. And so I have to ask myself, what of another agreement with you, another week of this? Another month? Another life? The record turned to noise long ago.'

With this Ollneek irradiated a demoralizing luminescence, the doorways to the descending halls bellowed and opened; a red hue from the depths of dead heart, a cosmic vacuum intuited, a descension of all surrounding matter to the lowest hum; for Ollneek all had become afterthought before this act of innocent insolence.

'Young boy! Let me show you what it is to be truly lost!'

Ollneek's penetrating posture of despondency sought all the young man had. Reaching to the point of internal infinity in every direction, it suffocated all remembrance of life.

Targeting head and heart as one, Ollneek lunged in a fit of miserable rage down the hallway, which, at that moment, stretched out in an impossible linear loop.

~

To the young man's right entered a colleague of mine; restful light with no need for battle dispersed static illusion, the bakery laid bare.

'Hello young man, be not afraid, you have nothing to fear, for I am only passing through.'

He turned to Ollneek who had disappeared, returning to his office. Fear subsided, and unyielding heat gave way to cordial warmth, sinking as honey into the young man's body.

'I am here on behalf of upstairs, I don't believe we have ever had the pleasure of working with you up there, and during my past annual reviews you seem to have not been available.'

'Annual reviews? I'm sorry, who are you?'

'You have nothing to be sorry for. Once a year the management reviews everyone in the company to see how they're doing, and you may be surprised to know, we have not forgotten you-'

'When you say everyone?'

'Indeed, even Old Nick - what is it you call him, Ollneek? Yes, well, we try. He has been around a long time, and has yet to appear for a single review.'

'I see, sorry, do continue.'

'Firstly, there is nothing to worry about. I am from head office, the area manager technically, but do not let that concern you, it is just a review, no big changes just yet. Now, I must ask, what is it you like to be called? We have a name on record, but often people prefer something else...'

'My friends call me...I don't know exactly, sorry.'

'Not the bother, it will come later, of that I am sure. You're here now and that is what matters. Before we begin, what was all that with Old Nick, an argument?'

'Something of the sort, he keeps trying to persuade me - or re-persuade me - of something I can no longer agree with, but for a long time did.'

'And what was it you once agreed with?'

'I couldn't tell you, it's all such a tangle, and now I feel that such an infinite knot is only a veil to conceal a nothingness beneath.'

'Practically speaking, what was the disagreement about?'

'I feel a tad foolish telling you this, especially considering your position, but it's regarding my job - at least as I see it.'

'What about it?'

'I don't know what it is I do, and yet it brings me only misery.'

'And if that is the case, then what exactly do you think is *wrong* down here?'

'It is not, firstly, a case of definite wrongness, but that nothing feels right. It isn't the error which is overt, but the diversion and alteration from how things *should* be.'

'And what, then, would constitute 'right' for you?'

'Perhaps right or correct are not the best words, and as for your question, I don't know what would constitute 'right', but it is not this.'

'And as for your job, what is it about it which no longer fulfills you?'

'Fulfills is an apt word, yes, Mr. - sorry, I never got your name...it's been so long since anyone has been down here...'

'Don't worry about such things, I wish to know about this job of yours.'

'Well, there is little to no work to speak of, I spend my days mulling-over decisions, second guessing life itself, always caught up in something. I am supposed to be baking but I couldn't tell you the last time I even set my eyes on a batch of bread. And yet something keeps me here, like a negative-nostalgia. All memories once green have soured, and my reason has become bitter. I feel I should not be admitting this to you, and yet something draws me to do so. All that Ollneek reels on about, it's all amounted to nothing, everything down here is a self-justifying circle, and there is a fear in stepping outside of these spheres of comfort.'

'What would your ideal alternative be?'

'I don't know much about upstairs. Honestly, I don't know. Just not here.'

'Perhaps I should ask you again, what is so wrong about this place? Take your time.'

'It is disorientation itself, a ship without anchor or helmsman within a sea of empty-passions, controlled only by nefarious and unidentifiable winds. It's to perpetually yearn for an elsewhere always out of reach. I wish to *know* that which I *feel* is Good and right, even if it means to suffer in other ways. For the work here, it's empty, and yet strangely difficult.'

'Difficult?'

'It is not easy, and yet it is not hard in the general sense. Nothing can be molded or grasped, everything is fleeting and dissipates upon definition; it is a labyrinthine transparency. And so it is easy to let go and do nothing, but if you wish for more, it is almost impossible to find a foundation to begin from, and so, it's difficult in the sense of standing upright.'

'I understand. Fear not, I shall return, but for now I must leave. I know we have work better suited to you, I shall be no more than a few days. In the meantime, I advise you to sort your affairs here. As for Ollneek, in time you'll come to understand him a little more, both for better and worse, I'm sorry to say.'

~

Was but a moment on a day like any other, and as all seconds can be catalysts for both hope and despair, this one heed the call, and from within a caesura of time I saw where I was for what it was, water washes the dust from my eyes, and I wish only to see more. And still, this too, faded, and years could pass, but the memory of this rupture remained, a fort of retreat in times of coldness. A place seated deep *of* me, a space of dispelling, vision changed and the bakery began to appear as just that.

~

The monotony of misery is its own worst enemy, to become disillusioned with disillusionment itself; how to stop this cycle which had come to define identity itself, I couldn't take an empirical step, nor make any decision, for both would have been made from the only language I knew, and so I made reserved attempts to *open* myself, to try accept what could be - if nothing were to happen, and nothing were to change, then all would remain the same; a terminal skepticism born from the transparency of passions, which sought to distrust the promises of the solely material; suspicion of unalloyed consumption taken to such a limit that after a final bitter whimper, it breaks, allowing the understanding self to come forth. Something pooling within a hidden recess of being, a welcomed earthy incandescence.

~

And time continues on, that is all my time still does, continues. It is void of quality, quantity reigns. What could have been days or weeks has bled into a ceaseless blur of fragmented events, and unsourceable memories; life *passes-by* as something not to be grasped, but to be immediately missed. To touch anything was to witness it already a few feet away.

The bakery never changed, no one peered in, and Ollneek kept a keener eye. He seemed present most days at the moment, running the show more methodically than usual, I sensed him ready to pounce on even my most minor slip-up. At times it appeared as if what was once a passion for him - running the show down here - had become a chore. Most he said, passed-through without need of his advice, a quick quip was enough to send them on their way; but those of potential merit were a struggle which led in the other direction, and he said we were very few indeed. He spoke of the idea of becoming not new, but that which one was all along...but he can never muster much of an ending, only that for him this place was needed for such changes. Sometimes I no longer understand him at all, it's as if he is speaking literal nonsense.

~

Never updated, never changing, forever unsettled, the bakery was a constant of liminal time; an anomaly of all creation, each act here was entirely out of joint from anything that made True sense. Ollneek has found his calling here, and exacerbates this fact as a means to make one feel a deep guilt at not attending to their own, as if such a thing is simply *afforded* one, as granted. Ollneek is a friend of old brick; many arrive, and a few go, such careers tend to grab, such walls suffocate, and such atmospheres justify themselves with no emotional backing. To lose focus is the norm, inattention the default, repetition a migraine; all retreats here are to the reason of an attention-deprived head, never to heart. In these walls you are told about, and shall believe from your own experience, of a world turned inside out and upside down, where there can be no such thing as a compass; virtue is vice, and vice is virtue, here error can only compound.

In disagreement with these walls I have had to address an in-between of reality which is in stark contrast to all that surrounds; but how can it be so difficult to believe in the simple? I wish to no longer confuse complexity with coherence, and understanding what it *is to* be, for *being* itself; I wish I could merely *see.* The external has all the traits, and is more often than not triumphant, but the glory of the internal is within a present never-tethered to spatial movement; a present that takes no account of empires falling or seasons changing - a courage to speak to that something here and now - I wish it could speed up from wherever it is, for I feel I can get no closer.

~

Time had become restless, emptiness itself, nothing even to fill. I had been without work, duty and task as far back as I could recall, but the present had ceased to produce even the pretension that anything could be done; I needed something, anything - I headed to Ollneek's office, something I hadn't done since I had arrived. I decided to head in-

'Mr. Ollneek?'

'-Boy! Is that you? Do not come in! What is it you want?'

'Well, Sir, I don't have any work to do.'

'Count your blessings, some would kill for such freedom. Wait for the next order to come in and be gone.'

'I haven't a clue when that will be, Sir.'

'Take some time off then - check the stockroom or freezer - why bother me, you're a competent lad.'

'You are my boss, I thought you'd need to know I wasn't busy.'

'My job isn't to keep you busy, just to keep you occupied! Just need to tick the boxes, no damned effort needed!'

'You don't mind if I'm doing nothing all day?'

'Have I ever complained about this before now? No, do what you will!'

'But I have *nothing* to do.'

Ollneek remained silent.

~

The interior wall of my millennia of malicious fortitude acts with sincerity for a mere second, and from the eye of a needle, a light year away, something reaches down into the openness; to question the idiocy of continuing to run a trail which has already ruined many limbs. I know I have received the message of all given earthly passions, I wish to hang up now and return to another conversation.

~

'What is going on in here, quite the racket?'

'Nothing, I'm here, as usual.'

'Watch that tone with me young'n.'

The young man ignores Ollneek

'Young boy, what is going on, something not right with you?'

'It doesn't matter...it is not something you would understand.'

'Tell, tell. Not only am I your boss, I am also your friend.'

'Ever since I had the discussion with the area manager...I've just been thinking, that's all.'

'What you thinking?'

'Nothing easy to explain, tough to articulate.'

'You tell me though, I need to know.'

'I've been thinking about this place, the bakery-'

'Your home, your home, all good here. No need-'

'There is a *need*, there is.'

'Well you explain then young'n, go ahead.'

With this Ollneek turned crimson, his darkness imbuing even the brickwork.

'It's the question of choice. In fact, this has always been *the* question.'

'No choice, you are you, and you are here - can't be simpler!'

'I won't allow this anymore.'

'Boy!-'

'No, Ollneek. I must speak, I must explain, for your methods of explanation fill the air with an empty density which only continues because of incessant refills, your voice a vacuum spouting language from and of the abyss, I cannot stand it any longer.'

'Ah! Do tell 'bout choice then! Lies I say-'

'Choice is the only constant, the foundation of all action. But here I have been led into the greatest tyranny of all. For I have not been *led into* the bad choice, the wrong choice. But have been broiled within it to such a degree, over such a long time, that it has begun to intrude into my very being, convincing me it is the one and only reality, the one and only choice. Firstly you lead astray, and secondly you convince others that there are no other paths, and so one becomes lost in a place seemingly bereft of all exits!'

'What choice, what path - where else you go?!'

'I do not know where I should go, but it mustn't be here. I shall tell you Ollneek, I have followed your advice throughout the atmosphere of this wretched place for a lifetime, and it has been a lifetime lost; I have given myself over to the false eternity of sour-repetition, and it is due to the thickness of this malevolent fog that I seek clean air, I must breathe. To repeat the 'functions' of base animality time-and-time again, to duplicate desire unto the last, as if just one more splurge will finally scratch the itch - but it is not an itch of matter or material, all your promises born from this brick and mortar don't even suffice to make it to the starting line of Goodness; the language you speak has no words for the feelings found in my heart; when you try and speak of Love, Goodness, Truth, Joy and Glory, you flatten them into structures of your own creation, entirely alien to their root; you seek to disprove Love with lust and Goodness with greed, and yet at their cores, these realities are born from different kingdoms!'

'Pah! Love, what ridic-'

'No more from you!'

Ollneek arose from the end of the corridor, turning to a pure blackness he struck along all lines, enveloping his kingdom, the entire was blind!

'From *me?* What I do? I only help. Ungrateful, ungrateful.'

'All you are *possible* of doing is lying, one can hear nothing from you which is not at least a mutation or a deceit of existence itself!'

'Tell, tell! What I say that is lie? Give me your best, boy!'

'The more time I give unto you, the more I lose - it is a danger to even humor your words. One last gasp for old times' sake...*as they say*...Old Nick. What is it you have offered me exactly? Laziness, selfishness, scorn, passions, and nihil - traits which lead one to the bitterest of veins, and for what?'

'I offer freedom, the greatest of all gifts. And you wish to give it away, for what, vague intuition?'

'Freedom cuts both ways, of which you speak only for a single path.'

'Worry not about the blade, turn on its side and it mirrors all desires!'

'You look past the reflection, to the self, and in illusory imagination cease all efforts to reflect. You offer a singular freedom, void of its negative double; action without consequence.'

'You speak nonsense, I not listen.'

'Even though you cannot *hear*, you must listen - You offer gluttony and ignore health, promiscuity yet suffocate love, self-abuse with ignorance of self, theft without neighbor, jealousy which assumes ego; in short, you offer a world void of other souls! What you have to give has been tried here, and it has failed, and so, you have nothing more to offer.'

'Pathetic, you could have been master, now you only slave, forever!'

'I Am, yes. Master of women, slave to desire; master of money, slave to greed; master of beauty, slave to vanity - and as for you, you are a master of hate, and a slave to pride.'

'You speak of choice, of truth and hate, whatever, whatever, useless, useless. This mean one thing of importance alone, *I* am always choice.'

'This I have accepted, and unfortunately, you are needed, in a way. Without thought of supporting this wretched place, how would I ever know what *not* to do.

The young man found himself without sight, without touch, falling in all directions at once; his Being at the limitrophe of a thousand eternal deaths.

'Where you go, this home!'

'He will come with me.'

The area manager arrived. All which was wicked vanished to the nothingness it called home; the young man, restored to life, stood calmly before my colleague.

'That is, young man, if you wish to do so?'

'I do.'

And with this, my colleague gestured towards the door which now streamed with light. The young man opened it tentatively, dared not look back, and slowly left the bakery.

~

I cannot make that moment out to be a grand act, but this should not deter hearts which seek to open in a meek quietness, for such is not a display of theatrics, but a deafening inner silence, a cacophonous appeasement; acceptance beyond all pretension, towards the possibility of reality.

To be disillusioned and thus to return to what is right is a matter of material fatigue; the world tried, the world failed; despite its best efforts, without Revelation, the language of material can never transcend, stuck within a symbolism of flesh. Bakery vanished, and my heart beat as if in a panic as to scare away the dust.

~

My colleague sought only to retrieve the young man, and yet Ollneek, settling to a low ebb, called to him.

'It should be no surprise to me that you're still working upstairs-'

The Messenger turned, scanning into Ollneek. He told the young man not to worry, for he would soon be with him, and with that closed the door of the bakery, shutting himself in. Staring at Ollneek the messenger remained silent.

'-nothing to say. You always were sanctimonious, from the first to the last.'

'Indeed, I am *still* upstairs, as you say, and I see that *you* are *still* down here. And what name is it you are going under now?'

'Not of your concern.'

'I overheard the young man call you Ollneek, or Mr. Ollneek, is it? You were always one for titles, had quite a few over the years I seem to recall - Light-Bringer, Father of Lies, Satan, *The* Devil, Lucifer, Old Nick - though that last one seems to have died out - and now, Oll-neek, get lazy did we?'

'Enough of this! You had best leave!'

'Or has Old Nick started to stick, become a little too well-known, a change was in order to try and make what can never be, be new?'

'Times change. I mold myself to them, as you know. And sometimes, they mold themselves to me, I've been doing quite well in that regard this past half century.'

'And this plasticity of yours is likewise the chain which keeps you bolted to this place.'

'...you speak of Truth, I spit on it!'

'And there are those that spit on you...'

'Numbers dwindling, though?'

The Messenger remained quiet.

'Do not think me such a fool as to not notice the increase of those coming my way. *Gracing* my brick walls with their vacuous presences. I know the passions greater than any, and I know they are on the rise, the tide has forever been in my favor, all runs *downward.*'

'We stood side by side at one time, those days of creation resonate eternal, and that light has not dimmed, and yet the bliss of that infinite expanse of light is lit within my being by a single event-'

Ollneek transformed into a writhing chaos, unsensible black and red hues bounding against all.

'-you remember it then, the day you fell, I half-wondered if you were so arrogant as to try to forget it entirely. Time is quite the muddle you know, we all push our past in front of us, and are pushed by our hopes for the future. For the prideful this is quite the curse, stuck between seeming failure and insignificance. And yet I must add, the imagery of that day remains vivid in the memory of all heavenly bodies; a crack on the horizon, a caesura within the fabric of fabric as the Angelic hordes looked below and bore witness...there falls he who believes in the possibility of undoing, of pride ad infinitum, pride as telos. I myself caught only the audible thunder of pure righteousness, as a pinprick of red broiled faintly beneath all perfection - What lies below, in time, can only bolster the Glory of the Above; your attempts will only ever be just that, attempts-'

'And yet you cannot explain the droves which pass me by!'

'There are those who *pass-by* you, indeed, and yet this place, now, and since I can remember, has a perpetual echo, with a resonation of but a solitary voice.'

'Many are out on errands, working overtime, this era rife with great potential.'

'I'm sure it is.'

'So it is the same question as ever, who shall prevail...'

'Your vision is collapsed in on itself, your sight is only recursive. All preachers have their respective choirs, but yours soon finds it can retreat no further than itself; it is not a question of who *shall* prevail, but of Who already *has* prevailed. For what were you ever to do against He; you think that not all darkness of creation is but a shadow and thus, being shadow, each abyss must contain a seed of light; darkness is limitation itself, light - though often shy, as per its character - is abundance. This, old commander of War, is the reason you shall forever fall; that which fuels your works consistently undermines their ends, you cast yourself out during each step; pride denies all sincere catharsis and forgiveness, nothing you touch can be content. Oh, dear Ollneek, my pity for you reaches far, father - still - of deception, and at the end of all days only one shall be deceived. You look upon these visitors as stock and fodder for a War already lost, further chaos developed leads only more towards the light; you may know their desires, but we know their hearts; from your position the sight of Love can never be granted, for it is something only given as a grace to those who wish to open to it. In your midst, even within your negative-presence, Love is mutated, it becomes a slave and thus disappears.'

'We go round in circles.'

'Mine has an end.'

'Enough, leave.'

'I shall, I must work.'

The Messenger slowly began to turn to the door, keeping his eye on Ollneek, briefly turning back.

'Before I go, a final question?'

'You always were incessant. Go on.'

'Do you truly not recall the splendor?'

'I recall only groveling, bending knee and whim; I recall a kingdom run incorrectly, I recall the absurdity of joy-'

'Farewell Ollneek.'

Looking upon Ollneek with a deep pity, The Messenger left the bakery, closing the door behind him.

PART 2: THE SHOP FLOOR

Upon exiting the bakery, The Messenger was to find the young man overwhelmed, his clothes hanging heavy on his shoulders, and short of breath.

'It may be a bit much at first, but it shall get easier, in a way, in time.'

'Where exactly are we?'

'Nowhere special, only where one is meant to be, that is, somewhere with firm ground.'

'It is rather...solid, weighty.'

'Very good, but much to do.'

'But *where* are we?'

'The ground floor, where else would we be?'

'I don't know.'

'Acceptance of uncertainty is good.'

'Surely not?'

'None so lost as those certain in their errors; those who despite becoming a cyclic friend to misery, never seek to question the repetition itself, as you yourself were able to do. But for now, let's keep things simple.'

'So, what am I to do...I still don't even know your name?'

'Do not worry, you have nothing to fear with me young man. Let us find out what you are to do, which itself is something you shall work out of your own accord, in a way. I shall be around, as will others, for now I must bid you farewell. Head around the corner, your vocation will find you.'

'When shall I see you again, where are you going?'

'Hopefully we shall meet again soon, and I am going to work.'

'I feel I owe you.'

'Consider it already repaid. Farewell for now.'

With that, the young man blinked, and The Messenger was gone.

~

The young man was then standing on the shop floor. For once, it felt, for him, though not immediately, that there was ground; there was no longer as much possibility to drift.

Before me a basic shop, a retail store. Though entirely *right*, the shelves are empty, and the space is quiet. Leaning against a clear section of wall, I notice silence for what it is, allowing it to overcome me. The lighting here casts clear shadows, there are limits and definitions in both time and space. A moment's rest, but that was all, but it was remembered in an instant, the potential to stop and breathe, to embrace the peace found Above all things.

'Hello there. I believe you are who I am to be training?'

'Excuse me?'

'I was to meet someone here who had just arrived from the bakery, I believe that is you?'

'I just arrived, yes...someone came and got me, though I'm not sure if it is me you are looking for.'

'I was told you called the area manager? You're here now, that's what matters.'

'I called?'

'Yes. We did try to call for some time, but our line could not get through, too much interference it seems. Now, do you *want* to be here?'

'I believe so, yes.'

'Then why overcomplicate things, it could all be so clear.'

'I'm sorry, it's just...I still feel a little lost, is all.'

'For now, do not worry about anything. Soon enough we'll get you to work. Now, I need to explain to you how things work up here. Let me show you the break room, and where my office is.'

The young man was led to the other side of the store where it opened into a side room, with a corridor off to the left. On the right of this corridor, halfway down, the break room, and finally, directly at the end, the office.

'And this is where I am, if you need help or guidance with anything all you need do is ask - you know where I am now.'

The young man entered the office alongside the second Messenger. Inside was only a single filing cabinet, two chairs, a desk, a notepad and a pen. There was a small window too, looking down onto the town. The young man began to look around the room.

'So...what is it you want to talk to me about?'
'Why it is you are here.'
'-Oh, I'm still not so sure.'

'It wasn't a question, the answer is clear to me - and to the area manager - it will become clearer, to you, in time. I'm here, in part, to help reveal.'

'I am sorry, I really do not understand.'

'You will, and strange as it may seem, you already do. First, I need to explain to you what you will be doing.'

'I have some experience here and there.'

'Do you? What exactly was it you used to do?'

To the young man's surprise his memory had deserted him, what he could discern of times gone past made no sense.

'...but, I know I have worked.'

'Perhaps as a child, but not in recent years, I've seen your file.'

'My file? Like a record of my life and deeds...can I see it?'

'Young man, you *are* your file. The only new information you could possibly garner from viewing it is that which you currently ignore, and thus would still ignore if it were in front of your face.'

The young man looked bemused.

'Young man, the day you can read your file in its entirety is the day you have no need to see it; if you can see all of yourself, as it should be, then you've no need to see.'

'Then why keep it at all?'

'Because it isn't for you.'

'But they are *my* words, *my* actions...'

'And they speak *of* you, and *for* you. Anyway, let's talk about what you'll be doing.'

The Messenger handed the young man a concise schedule of daily tasks, with an attached sheet of various rules and regulations.

'More to come, I'm afraid, but as they grow, they simultaneously become less.'

'Well, I think I understand the work side of things.'

'But 'Why so many rules and regulations' you ask?'

'...yes, how did you know I'd ask that?'

'That's what they all ask, it is the common first question of all men during all occasions 'Why can't I do what I want, when I want?''

'All? There are others, from where?'

'Yes, there are others who have been here before you. Some from the bakery such as yourself, others need a refresher in their vocation.'

'Others from the bakery?'

'Of course, why wouldn't there be? You are here, after all. Anyway, your question regarding 'the rules'?'

'I guess my question is, how can such a place thrive under such conditions?'

'Firstly, not everyone and everywhere has to 'thrive', as you put it. For many it is a triumph to lead a simple existence. Likewise, for one *to thrive* is more often than not for others to be deprived, if one is thinking of thriving in that common worldly sense. Anyway, this is not our focus. Foremost one must ask why there are rules at all? It is an outright lie that such obedience is asked solely for the purpose of restricting freedom, and they only seem so gratuitously abundant if one exclusively seeks that which is forbidden, which, as you can imagine, is prohibited for Good reason. If one is to look at the sheet once more, one will notice a list no longer than one's hand, and yet you act as if all shall end? What, one may ask oneself, is the worry?'

'But in what way can a limitation allow one to grow, to become better, surely this is all quite stifling?'

'You can call them rules, you know.'

'Ok, how do so many rules simply not just end up stopping freedom and creativity?'

'You have missed an important question, tucked away in your own inquiry - what is it to be free? Unfortunately, despite everything this eternally-modern world may tell you, freedom can never exist in a vacuum, there is no such thing, on this earth, as pure-freedom. Freedom without consequence does not exist.'

'This is a conclusion I have experienced and understood in abstract, but what does it mean in practice?'

'Now that is a great question, and one I would urge you to remember. If one is to think of any freedom - innocent, naive, malicious, modern, traditional, large or small, it has its opposite; freedom is always freedom *from* something; each free act contains both a dark core and a liberating light; never free, only free *from*.'

'So all freedom is an escape from something worse?'

'Not quite, it shall become clear to you in time, and it is not for me to spell it out. As is the case with your personal file, without the experience of understanding, I could show you Truth and you wouldn't recognize it for what it was. Freedom to laze around, be rude, be selfish etc. these are all freedoms, self-imposed rules which have become so habitual they appear as truth, of course, they are not. I have read in your file that you recently proclaimed 'Freedom cuts both ways'?'

'I think I recall.'

'It is a shame your memory is how it is, for you saw only half the Truth it seems. Let me ask you, is the glutton free? Is the promiscuous man who is unable to truly connect to anyone free? Is the addict's individual freedom a *real* freedom? I shall let you decide, but here you are asking 'what is freedom?' And this is something I cannot tell you, you must work it out.'

'I think I would like to know.'

'Wouldn't we all, but I cannot push you to the end. Freedom is of a certain decision, one explainable only by the heart of the faithful. If I were to tell you *how* to be free, you wouldn't be, in fact, you *couldn't* be; all the freedoms of the modern man are in this vein, selected by voices which always escape capture. All *that*, that which you used to partake in, the nothingness, the not-caring, from where did it arise? Who told you that was the thing to do, the way in which freedom is found? All of this is beside the point, young man, I cannot walk for you, but I will certainly help you in your stride, but that first step...that's yours.'

'And when am I to take that?'

'As I have been saying, you have taken it, you just need to learn to see.'

'Ok. Could we go back to the rules?'

'Sharpened throughout time - rules, regulations, I-shall-nots, tradition, there are many names. In relation to what we were just speaking of, these rules are a toolkit to protect us from debts, mistakes and weights, they save us from missing the mark. In short, rules cut a lot of self-justifying off at the root. Rules, if explained correctly, both articulate where the rot arose, and provide an antidote to stop it spreading ever again. Tell me, where you arrived from, were there rules?'

'Sure, but they were never followed..nor mentioned for that matter.'

'...did ignoring these rules cause any consequences?'

'Not that I remember.'

'If one breaks the rules, and there are no consequences...there are no rules. And so, without limitation, what is anything? You cannot even sit without the limit of a chair. Nothing can be accomplished without a limit, something to move *towards*, or to move *from*; without any limits man is simply unimaginable, he'd be lost; a maze without entry, exit or path.'

'Quite the fate.'

'Maybe for some, possibly for none, I cannot say.'

'So there will be rules whilst working here, that's what this paper is?'

'Again, I advise reading that sheet, and understanding why such rules have arisen. There *are* rules, yes. As to whether you hold to them, this is your choice.'

The young man quickly scanned the sheet, still looking confused.

'If rules are followed only out of terror of punishment, as opposed to a true understanding, then they are not *followed* but feared, and in moments of supposed seclusion would therefore be abused and avoided altogether. For the beauty of the Truth behind rules and tradition is that when it comes to sensible people, they will uphold the Law, not for fear of punishment, but solely in the name of the Good and the True. Let us say there is a rule which if broken means the perpetrator suffers pain, or misery?'

'Yes?'

'Do you believe those who break such a rule would regret doing so?'

'Well, of course.'

'But why, because the rule was broken? Or because of the punishment? - For now, the answer doesn't matter, something to think on.'

'And if I *do* break a rule?'

'*If?* Young man, if you proceed through these days without breaking one rule, then we shall switch places. But, if you are to break a rule then I advise you only to be sincere and honest about what it is you have done, even if not with me, at the very least with yourself; to lie to oneself is a troublesome pit. Allow the consequences of such mistakes to bolster the original reasons for obedience; in short, be sure to learn your lesson. Follow them, for now, as best you can.'

'And what am I to do? I took a quick glance at the schedule, it says I am to mop the floor three times a day, is that it?'

'Is that it, he says. For now, that is all.'

'And who do I report to?'

'Whomever you feel like reporting to, but rest assured I shall be keeping an eye.'

'I must admit, I feel rather fragile before all of this.'

'Nothing here is seeking to break you. But I understand, for this is not uncommon. You feel this way for reasons which will become clear, once again, in time. One last thing, down the hallway, to the right - we passed it on our way here - is the break room, I recommend popping in once a day.'

~

The young man got up from the slightly padded seat and looked past The Messenger to a calendar on the wall. He couldn't discern the date, but he felt, for now, this didn't matter, perhaps in time it would. For the present was calling, and to lean on either side would be to avoid listening, hearing that Someone who was right there. Walking to the door to The Messenger's office, he looked back, he was no longer there, he understood he was simply to move on.

Entering the hallway, the door closed behind him with a subtle click. He was on his own. Aside from the sounds of various appliances and the general humdrum of movement, the store was still. Still enough to unnerve those who were not ready, and yet, settled enough to allow fog to disperse, if one allowed it.

The young man's only task was to mop the floor, thrice a day; a task, which as all tasks, could be performed lazily or with effort; he felt, and thus knew - whether accepted or not - that as one thing is done, all things are done. Excuses did not last long there.

And here I was, with a clear task, simply to mop. I wish to try and get my bearings, to allow this growing circle to develop into a full compass. Walking past the shelves, I see them clearly only when close-by, even the floor appears only when I apply a strained attention.

The young man walked directly to the front of the store. Before him were set three huge windows looking out onto the town. Nowhere close to a city, but far from a village. One might say that people may even take a day trip here, but then, what is a day after all? It had the hustle-and-bustle of men and women, a somewhat pleasant affair. Not so for the young man.

I can see, but only vaguely, perhaps ten feet in front of me, sometimes a little less, sometimes a little more; but my vision struggles for anything beyond immediacy. If I strain I can hold the front of the store in thought as a unity, three large windows and a basic stone doorway. As I look out of the windows, the horizon assembles only as an impermanent line, holding but the width of a coin in vision. Something has fallen...is falling away, and its replacement is built of hesitancy. I must be patient and work with what I have, here and now.

Some time went by in that state, the young man's eyes fixed fast to the floor, focusing only on the most basic of tasks; he was to learn to walk again. One could notice him getting along quite plainly - but as many have recorded, it is a rare part of the psyche of men which records when things are going smoothly. This, of course, is much to their benefit, for smooth sailing doesn't make for an experienced sailor; what this young man sought was still the More, and tensed before the most simple of actions in a manner of condescension, ignorant of the fact that the More which he sought can be found both at the highest mountain peak, and within the lowest gutter; he desired to poke those wounds of life which if left alone become wondrous, and yet if prodded with an impetuous nature become yet sorer and more bitter.

Staring over the top of simplicity, the young man began to idle at his mop, and ponder and ponder, as many do. Questions too big for the mind get caught up in their own tangle, the question 'Who am I?' taken without thought for relation, or 'What is the meaning of all this?' viewed solely from the perspective of the questioner. The young man is forgiven of such inquisition of course, for the shop is for such problems. Those employed here are vetoed thoroughly, but as for custom, of that - as with any shop - we have no control, and it is not our duty to deter custom, only to teach one to recognize it for what it is, and act accordingly; countless definitions of the good and the bad lead one only to constrain Truth and Goodness, conflating them with temporal actions, as opposed to virtuous eternal emanations.

And yet for his idling and questioning (the latter often solved with a cessation of the former), the young man kept to his task, to his duty; his mind, however, did wander, and his heart indulged. He could have got lost, and yet his feet were firm, which the shop quite adored. We would have run to him, of course, if he so wished.

~

I had found an intermittent peace, and in its absence it left an eternal trace, a place where one could always return. And yet, I struggle here and now, not with the tasks at hand, which are their own, but of articulation. Before, of what I can remember, there was a vastness to language, a tyranny of the subjective word. But here, in open spaces, there are no interjections of the alphabet, description blooms only in secret; from here I say, that I seek what cannot be said.

~

Some more days passed by, as they do for men. The passage of time was new for the young man, for the passing of time only matters if there is something one cares about growing, even if it is silent or seemingly forgotten; without hope for the future, the passing of time can be nothing but a material vessel to either be grieved, or filled with empty delights.

It was some time before a customer ventured to the store - long forgotten, it seems. Attending to his tasks, which quickly became routine, the customer asked him a simple question –

'Excuse me!'

'I'm sorry?'

'Huh? Do you work here?'

'...I suppose so, yes.'

'Well, do you, or don't you?'

'Yes, yes I do.'

'Very well then, could you tell me where the coffee is?'

'I'm sorry, but I can't actually, no. I mostly just-'

'I thought you said you worked here?'

'Well yes, but-'

'And yet you don't know where such a common item is?'

'That isn't my job-'

'What is your job then? To *not* know things?'

'Just to mop and clean up, for now.'

'Sounds about right!'

And with that the customer was gone.

For some time, a quality of time, opening internally, the young man thought often of his customer, and, a short time after, on a day lighter than others, the young man was abruptly introduced to the store manager.

Her presence flowed with a delicate ease over all within sense, rhythm softened, and the store became alleviated of a tension hidden since time began. I retained attention to my mop, but I was relieved by a kindness of spirit I'd never known. In simple speech, with a fragile accent, she spoke to me.

'Hello young man. Now, what is this I have heard about you being a little rude towards customers?'

'I'm sorry...excuse me?'

'Some time back I was told, you were a tad rude to a customer, is this true?'

'I'm sorry, I don't know who you are?'

'I've been told you love to ask questions, but that doesn't matter right now, just let me know if you were rude.'

'I remember now, a single customer, yes. Was a quick exchange.'

'So you do recall?'

'Yes, but I was not rude.'

'And you are sure this is true?'

'I believe so, yes.'

'Very well then.'

'Ok. So, who are you?'

'It's really no matter and changes little, but I am the manager of the store, and I have been told a lot about you. All this aside you are needed in the office. The area manager is there, just so you are aware.'

'They wish to see me now?'.

'Why else would I tell you, off you go.'

~

All this passes, if I let it, quite simply. Two had come so far, practical and helpful, and there was warmth from both, tough to accept for someone with a heart long since slave to tyrannical head. Yet now, brought forth and reaching within without knowledge of aggression, the source of tears, a rehabilitation of care. Each sentence a sigh, and all an invitation for a betterness built atop love alone. Where could this have been? A first act of appeasement, an admittance of Love lost as faculty; the past now belongs to a vision looped upon itself; the future belongs to eyes seeing only via the sight of heart.

~

The young man walked with slight trepidation to the office. Despite being told the area manager would be there, he was still surprised. For he could only recall him from the foggiest of memories.

'Young man, what a delight it is to see you here. I am told you are doing well, and I believe you two just met.'

'Yes indeed, she's very kind. And I believe I'm doing well, yes.'

'No, I am told you are doing well, and so you *are* doing well. Now, young man, we are to ask you something - why are you here?'

'...it doesn't feel exactly as if it was my choice, in the usual sense, I feel I *ended* up here.'

'And what is it to 'end up' somewhere?'

'I guess it is as it sounds, a passive act.'

'Is this truly what you believe?'

'I'm not sure how I feel. The last few...weeks? They have been quite intense.'

'Weeks? Young man, you have been here close to two years now, hence the meeting.'

'It has flown by-'

'Indeed, it has. Now, how are you *finding* it here - we ask that you are honest, for our records.'

'Truly, I can't remember where I was before - I *know* where I was, but the memories themselves are *of* that place, to connect to them in sympathy is to return. Things here work, things there do not. But here is also different in many other ways, my body has a weight to it and is yet lighter, and a fog is being lifted, slowly, from my eyes and everywhere.'

'And the tasks, your duties?'

'They are...simple, what I have needed for some time.'

'Simple?'

'It is just mopping and sweeping, is there more I am supposed to be doing?'

'And what exactly is so simple about such cleaning?'

'It is a basic task, a very clear task.'

'Clear, yes. But there is no such thing as a basic task.'

'May I ask how so? That nothing can be basic...'

'All tasks have an aim and end, however localized. If there is no such aim, or purpose, then something else entirely is employing you. There must be something More to all things, if you wish to see it, that is.'

'And so the aim of cleaning the store is...what, exactly? For there to be a clean store?'

'Is that where you develop your work...your purpose, *from?*'

'I work from somewhere very new. It feels as a breeze is underneath each movement and thought, light yet awe-inspiring-'

The young man hesitated.

'...go on.'

'It is easy to lose, it's fragile, delicate. And when I return from the break room, it is as if my feet are anchored, my hands can once again clasp, movements flow, and yet in time...I imagine, I fantasize of all manner of things, and with that the air dissipates, and then minutes, hours later I return to myself, knowing not where I have been; it is a plain-web-of-knots, which it seems I continually refuse to untangle by the mere act of letting go of the rope; it is the hardest of all things to give one's self over *not* to myself.'

'What is it which is within reach during this possible act of...*opening?*'

'...I wish I had the words, but I do not. It is for me and *of* me, and only for me.'

'And do you always want this elusive feeling?'

'Yes and no.'

'Continue...'

'With it comes a weight, to be anchored - of itself, not a problem, but, with such roots comes a form of responsibility. Not to anything in particular - to a degree it is to myself, but it is in relation to something unseen, something not yet, and something never accomplished.'

'And this is there underneath, within, as you attend to your duties?'

'Yes.'

'And so, that *basic* task of cleaning?'

'And that is the peculiar frustration, to know it will need to be repeated day after day, whilst fighting against the shattering of that delicate Voice. It deepens the task, making it not for itself. Can I admit such a thing?'

'Admit what?'

'That the duties feel like tests.'

'You cannot admit, only accept, as it seems you wish to. In what world is there an act which itself is *not* a test?'

'I do not follow.'

'Be it sweeping, resting, talking, or mere walking, each act can be *seen* and *used* in some manner - If one thing can be empty, so can all things - this being the definition of darkness. To purposely ignore the fragility of light, to lapse, be it willingly or ignorantly, is to lean into the flux of relativity, into chaos-out-for-itself. That which you describe as fragile will be so forever, and so a single act of carelessness towards its Nature means one could lose it eternally. Do you follow?'

'I follow. To devolve even the most seemingly insignificant moment is to damage value itself, leading meaning to entropy. Hard to return from there. As you say, lost eternally.'

'If that is the choice one makes, but even so, there is never such certainty in these things. It is good you follow, for now we shall not complicate matters further.'

'So I am making good progress?'

'Your work is of a redeemable quality, progress we can talk of another time - now, this customer we have been hearing about?'

'Yes?'

'Apparently you were rude to him?'

'I don't believe I was, I stated only what I knew.'

'Very good. Let us think of some further suitable work for you.'

'I am fairly comfortable sweeping, more than happy to stay there.'

'We know you're comfortable there, but we never said you were here for comfort, hence the change. We understand the checkouts will be a good place for you now, the ones by the window. Would this be something you will do?'

'That would be ok.'

'Good. Your new acquaintance will train you, and she is already waiting. Young man, it has been good to see you.'

~

And with that the young man exited the office to find the manager standing outside, a kindness waiting.

'Young man, it is wonderful to see you again, and I do hope that was fruitful. Now come along, we have things to be getting on with.'

'It has been such a long time since I have seen-.'

'That is for you, for then; and this is for us, for now.'

'Of course.'

'Very good, now let's head over to the tills.'

With that she took a swift lead ahead of the young man, her presence extending to each side of the aisle, a wash of beauty bringing forth color, swerving between customers which quickly disappeared from sight. Rarely did she need to look back to see if the young man was with her. They arrived at a set of three tills, facing out into the store, with a small door opening to them, the other end looking out onto the town via one of the large windows.

'What is it you'd like to ask, young man?'

'Where did all those customers come from?'

'They were always here, perhaps you did not look, perhaps it was otherwise. Don't let it concern you for now.'

'I don't fully understand?'

'Oh, what it would be to *fully* understand!'

'Do you not? Fully understand, that is?'

'Oh no, can't imagine I'd be managing such a store if I did.'

With that she opened the door to the checkouts, leading the young man to the one furthest to the end, directly in front of the window.

'All you do is stand here and serve the customers. Simple enough.'

'And how exactly do I work all this machinery?'

'Everyone asks how to work the machine, and not how to serve the customers. Both of these things shall work themselves out, in time.'

'So I stand, wait, and serve?'

'Young man, you shall do fine.'

'And will you be around if I need you?'

'If you truly *need* me, I shall already be here, if you wish it to be so.'

With that, she left the young man alone at the checkouts, slowly drifting out of sense with a polite farewell.

~

For some days, possibly weeks, I've been standing at this desk without the squeak of a single customer. I suddenly have a lot of time of my own, sometimes restful, sometimes noisy. I have the time to gaze out of the store window, out into the street. The roads a continual grey blotted shape, blurring into a faded horizon. I see no other workers, but something stirs here which applies a pleasant weight to all things; heels rooted, weather to weather. Around me, throughout this passage, the shelves slowly become filled, and the world too is now secretly audible...it is often even nice to listen to. More often than not I am content to just stand, without need for break or reason - happy to just be. It has been a lifetime since thought has been without battle.

I am still uncertain as to whether or not I have truly dealt with any customers at all, my memory is still a little hazy. Perhaps of most importance is the growth of all that surrounds, all is warmer, repetition itself fading away, each moment holding the potential to blossom within its own newness; my duty, without the habits of didactic finger-wagging, is only to adhere to these drops of light, giving myself over to all they have to offer, and in such an acceptance the good and bad transform into an empathy lost to Eden.

And moments finally arise where this vision of the in-between becomes praxis, the first custom I can say to have served, and in return a vision of the past-become-new, an unexpected thought assumed lost. He enters quietly, an energy sullen and overcast, purchases of no importance, and yet attended to the line with a noticeable calmness.

'Good morning young man.'

'Morning sir'

'And how are you then?'

'I have no need to complain.'

'No need? All must be very great indeed then?'

'Quite right, no need.'

'No thought of getting home...have you been working long?'

'I have been working for some time, yes. Hopefully I will return home soon enough.'

'Keep at it, and see you around.'

And with that I was drawn, by a momentous delicate orbit, to a vision of what could Be; the humble warmth of being, a lighting subtle and kind, free to play amidst reality; sight overcome with a wash of white and blue, cleansing all veils; and, if but for a moment, one's heart beats to a rhythm it has yearned for since birth. The word home once only toyed with my mind, creating various material imaginings, *houses* of brick and mortar, allowing only the rational rest at the end of toil and sorrow. But Reason comes forth battered and bruised, arm-in-arm with the Sacred, and all fantasies are burnt out by a righteous light, leaving, here-and-now, a trace of the only Rest there can ever be. Such a favor clings to the circulation of action, each step a reminder of what is to come - if only I seek to remember It, especially in times when It seems to never have been at all.

There may be what one could call a home-on-earth, a place of repeated rejuvenation, enough to suffice for a lifetime of wounds, itches and lacks, and yet seat within the True home removes all compulsion for desire itself, a final ontological sigh before a shift to completeness and harmony.

The man turned back to me, sending a smile, the feeling dissipated and the familiar reach of the new remained, a beacon of elsewhere; seed planted and stem grown, a help and thanks, a place to turn to in the darkness of deluded self.

From this place, I returned to the here-and-now with the attention of a twin-arrow which rebounds between the internal and external. Caught in this passage, one begins to know the empathy which was before all things. It was from here I could recall who I had *been*, errors and faults, malevolent ink clouding the pure-water of clarity itself; from this position I was shook to see the contrast of all which acts in the name of the Good as opposed to that of evil, in a word, forgiveness.

~

Some more time passed, I didn't mind how much, for it was not mine, and never was; when leant into, and not *used up*, temporality transcends self. A heart half-filled, one direction leads Home, the other to an infinite-misery.

I was still on the checkouts, there had been quite a few more customers - I even began to recognize some regulars. In time we greeted each other with various pleasantries, and yet also, I came to understand who to leave be.

As I looked to the town and the customers leaving, some would wave back to me, standing in my usual spot; a place of comfort and direction. It was an early evening, the starlight heavy on top of the town's buildings, a silence of Glory abounded, and peace seemed possible in all things, when the area manager came to visit me.

'Young man, a pleasure to see you once more. How are you doing?'

'I wasn't expecting you.'

'I know. Nice night out tonight, yes?'

'A very nice night.'

'And I am so glad you see it. The reason I am here, a small matter regarding your previous job.'

'You'd like me to go back to cleaning?'

'A little further back, young man.'

'I'm sorry, I do not recall.'

'I understand, perhaps it is that you do not - from such a position - wish to remember what once was. You arrived here from somewhere else, somewhere in this store, the bakery. Led by...'Ollneek', as you called him. He has left you a message in my office. It is there if you are to go look for it.'

'I'd best go read this message then, see what it is, at least, no?'

'If that is what you think is best.'

And so my mind was cast back into the labyrinthine fog, brick and grind, noise incessant, a low hum protruding into all joints; my being tapped on the door of arrogant disharmony once again. Memories pierced by shadow gained ground, not before root rose and a pale glare washed thought itself, a past revealed in lieu of present fragile hordes of Good. You see self-as-self, trembling between apathy and appeasement, the sincere falling rightward, the lost believing the left to be the only path.

'The message is on the desk.'

'What does it say?'

'It is not *our* message. It is for you, if you wish to accept it'

'It may be important. I guess I will take a look, for old times' sake at least.'

The young man turned over the small card.

'My boy, young'n - when you come back?'

'That's it?'

And with that, the phone rang.

'It's for you. It's Ollneek.'

'Ok?'

'Well, do you wish to speak to him?'

'I'll see what he has to say, his first message here made little sense.'

'Pick it up then.'

The young man picked up the receiver.

'Hello?'

'That you? That really you young'n?'

'It's me I guess, yes.'

'Guess? You not know who are?'

Ollneek let out a laugh he could only mimic.

'It is me, yes.'

'Wanted to speak for while, couldn't get through, where been?'

'Working here, upstairs. I quite like it. It makes sense.'

'You not belong there though, we make great team back then, no?'

'I don't remember all that much, really.'

'Such nonsense, boy. We had some great times, you not remember. You should think back.'

'Maybe, I don't know, I haven't thought about it for a long time. Anyway, why do you need me back?'

'Nothing is getting done boy, completely slack, all over place without you - could say I even miss you.'

'Well, I have work up here now, I'm doing quite ok too.'

'Ok, ok. Let's see, what kind of work they give you?'

'I'm currently on the checkouts, dealing with customers, before I was-'

'Pah! What folly! We used to talk about people, you forget our talks, my lessons, no?'

'I can't recall them this second, no.'

'People...people dear boy, cause of all misery. I bet they bore you no-end, I am sure of it.'

'I've never thought about it. Ollneek I-'

'Oh come now boy, that work isn't for you, those hours, restrictions and rules, that ongoing struggle they so love. Come back to me young'n, we made such a great team.'

'Ollneek, it was all repetition, and I have heard this before, it is...you are...predictable!'

'My boy, I know not what to say to such ungratefulness.'

'Answer me this - What *precisely* do you want from me?'

'I want nothing *from* you...I want-'

'I have to go.'

And with that the young man put down the phone, and turned the message back over.

'Well handled young man, though there was no need to get into such a discussion in the first place.'

'He had not crossed my mind in some time, he was somewhere else completely and yet for a short time, the bakery appeared to be here.'

'He is a strange one, Old Nick.'

'You know of him?'

'*Of him?* There isn't a soul who doesn't know him, and he know of them. As for myself and your other two acquaintances, we all go back with him a long time.'

'And what is the story there?'

'Rather apt young man to call it *the story,* for one may ask if there is any other? But I assume you are asking about Old Nick himself?'

'I think so.'

'There was a split...the longest time ago; a disagreement to end all disagreements; one side always-already defeated, the other eternally victorious - and yet Old Nick, he still tries, and as time exists, Old Nick shall be. That is how it is, and how it must be.'

'Must be?'

'Often the query to such a statement. Indeed young man, it *must be*. For all that you have opened yourself to, all which you understand as warmth and love, it cannot be without its contrary. That is to say, with admitted sadness, there cannot be Good without evil; for if one exists without the other each becomes quite meaningless. But it is between the two that choice is grown, for if either Good or evil ceases to exist there is no *choice*, and without such agency there is no freedom at all. It *must* be so, for one cannot love if it is forced, and one cannot have faith if it is made mandatory; it is in this *choice* where one's being can find the potential for fullness.'

'And his error?'

'He *is* error. Old Nick deludes himself, with pride as his primary fuel, both to use and beget; he believes his solipsism draws all to him, and yet the inverse is true. He is deluded in the subtle belief that he is unified, and yet just one mere look or talk with him from the sincere of heart is to see he is fragmented, perpetually lost to a thousand-thousand splintered desirous selves .'

'Can he ever be...healed, or...saved?'

'Where we were young man, back then, was before a Glory beyond all dreams of human-heart. Where you have what is called faith, we had - and eternally have - knowledge. And thus in the face of objective Truth, Old Nick *made* a firm choice; one based not on inability of *belief*, but of prideful arrogance.'

'I spent a lot of time with him, believing him, hanging on every word. I feel I should loathe him, and yet all I can muster is a deep pity.'

'You should speak to the manager about this.'

'Ok, I shall.'

'She also needs to discuss your work.'

'...ok.'

'Do not worry, young man. You shall be ok, and all shall be fine.'

~

She was waiting for the young man outside the office.

'I am told you have other work for me?'

'Something of the sort, yes. Come along.'

'We were talking about Ollneek.'

'Ah, that old fool.'

'They said to talk to you about him?'

She quickly halted between two aisles.

'What did they say exactly?'

'Only to talk to you about him...'

'Very well, I guess it is one of those times to tell such a tale once more. Follow me, we shall head over to my office.'

She led the young man back from where they had come, to the hallway. Then past the office, taking a previously unseen right-hand turn. Before them an old barn door, reaching high, out of space and time, emanating a rural weather pattern. She pushed it open with ease, holding it open for the young man.

'Come along, it is all quite safe.'

The young man stepped in. Before him a rural barn, the light seeping easily between the holes in its dated wood. Subtle boards covered the floor which held a stove and large varnished desk, covered in trinkets and bits of straw. Up the walls and along the supports books flowed as a current, with piles stacked throughout the barn's entirety. The young man missed this place, though he had never once been here. The

young man looked upon this barn's interior, bowled over by
calm.

'So you like it here?'

'Very much, but why is *this* here?'

'And why would it not be here, you only need to look, young man.'

'And this is your office?'

'It was chosen for me.'

'And what is it you *do* again?'

'I am just here to help, without payment. Difficult to believe nowadays I imagine, but I am entirely sincere. But I also teach people to see and hear, as we all do.'

'I think I understand. And so, what of Ollneek?'

'I haven't forgotten why we are here, young man, but for now, let's take some time; places like this are built for rest.'

~

It has been a while, I have been elsewhere I suppose. But now, this wonderful now, all is becoming as a summer spring, hidden under arching green, with a sound and sight revealed only to the patient. If the resonance of that serene Voice had not penetrated so deep, I would have thought to bellow with a laughable absurdity 'How can this be? Where has this been?' and yet, *it has*, and so I need not.

~

She was there, a presence throughout the barn, embracing all.

'So, let us talk of that old fool. I would assume, you being a human and all, that you wish to know it *all?*'

'Just some clarity on him, I guess.'

'Clarity, no. Not with him. There never can be, never could be. If Ollneek ever seems to make sense, then you are somewhere quite dangerous, and Lord forbid you have been hypnotised into thinking such a place is right, such is the double tyrannous nature of his tricks. A long time ago, Ollneek was...'high-up', Light-Bringer, he was called. But as you may know, he has had many different names throughout time, his latest, Ollneek, is but a modernization of his previous popular name, 'Old Nick', he is getting lazy it seems. Anyway, everyone knew him, and of him, and all was Glorious, unified, harmonious...*in* harmony. But this was not enough for him, despite all that he *knew*, it simply was not enough - there are no reasons for this neglect of Glory outside of his *own* pride; no reason nor understanding. In short, he believed *he* could *do better,* and now such an idea resonates throughout time in all his works - reform, mutate, divide, cut, sever, schism and break, all growths from the root of self-assumed superiority. Let me ask you something young man, where do you think one should focus their attention in the sentence 'This is good, but I can do better!'"?

'The idea of 'better''?

'But where does that idea arise from?'

'From someone, from a person?'

'Quite right. *I* can do better, they say. I, I, I, I, this is the sound which brings the world to its knees.'

'But what is wrong with simply having an opinion?'

'An opinion in the right place is mostly both harmless and pointless. But if all is made a certain way, by that Someone you are yet to fully speak with, then such propositions as *I can do better*, such that Ollneek made, can only ever be *im*perfect.'

'And Ollneek's form of 'better'?'

'It doesn't matter, and can never make sense. Ollneek is the father of lies, the one who seeks to delude others into thinking the already perfect needs perfecting, pure delusion. The first to create rivalry, jealousy, hate, envy and all of the below, but before all these was pride. He only sees existence as meaningful if one is in a position of superiority, and once one is at the top of one hierarchy - be it money, status, fame etc. - they seek the next, and the next, and the next, and on and on, until there is that one which they can never get above; Ollneek and all his works seek to do the impossible, to get above the Above.'

'And so what happened?'

'Quite the scuffle! Glory came upon them, the War of all wars, the War to begin war.'

'*Them?*'

'There were those who followed Ollneek, roughly a third. A third lost.'

'And yourself, where were you?'

'Amidst the fight, a battle of pure confusion, for Ollneek first...destabilizes. Near the end I found myself near him.'

'And?'

'I shall never forget turning to him, witnessing the purity of illusion and malice condensed to a near-perfect mask. But this vision of Glory he sought to mimic he could - and can - do so only externally, you look close enough and one can see a million cracks; such external Glory is to turn one's back on Grace - not as a mistake, but as a choice.'

'So, what happened?'

'Ollneek was outstretched before me, a pause of complete tension. The now eternal War of all creation centered itself into each soul alike. A flash and a strike and All came to our aid, sincerity my sword, with armor bolstered by hope. And, despite our perceivable closeness on that occasion, an abyss formed between the sides, a recognition of that which was Right from that which could never be. A shriek of heart, a retreat to warmth, as a fracture of light ruptured the horizon of existence itself. The hand of Ollneek transformed into a worn hoof, matted fur dripping grease - from the smoke protruded pure-flesh deformity, a writhing hatred allowed life; and with this, heaven split in time, and all that sought only itself alone fell to the pits of its own creation. A glaring black lacuna condemned throughout all time to never be filled. '

'And after that?'

'After that, all work, for all people's - Angels and fallen - began.'

'And so your work?'

'Ollneek and his followers *appear* in the in-between of all messages; I am a Messenger, they are static on the line, noise which seeks to alter the whisper. Ollneek is always in the middle of all communication, and so I am to teach one to use their senses in such a way that Grace becomes the sustenance of all harmony; for all is unfathomably delicate when it comes to the transfer of Love.'

'So you are here to teach me how to do so?'

'Not at first, there are many Messengers, we all have our roles. There's a lot of overlap.'

'I'm not sure I fully understand.'

'You say that a lot, it's nice. Young man, there are places where one cannot go with their boots on, and all wish to take them off, but the greatest struggle is firstly just to see them.'

'But we see ourselves all the time?'

'We only see who *we* wish to see, and rarely are we aware of who it is who's talking. The easiest lies to believe are the ones we tell ourselves.'

'So then I can only have one question - How *do* we see...for the first time? What *is it to see?*'

'I guess we should think of that for some time, for we have so much of it here.'

~

And so she and the young man sat for some time beneath the cascade of warm light, the last remnants of ancient straw glowing with patient incandescence. The young man occasionally stood, pacing along with a rhythm which never disturbed. Her presence ebbed and swelled, the young man always in overlap, within a tough safety born from awe. Seasons didn't wait, but their passing came without judgment, time itself resigned in the face of the sincere, and so it came to be that the young man took a seat on the floor, propped against the wooden desk.

~

Her voice, from nowhere, and somewhere.

'So, have we got any further towards being able to see? Being able to hear?'

'What a thing it would be to be able to say so with pure reason.'

'It can be confirmed, but only by you.'

'From the heart?'

'*Secretum meum mihi.*'

'...and so, seeing?'

'Young man, there is only so much I can give you; one cannot spell out Joy with words alone. There is but one place man can Be, and you have already *felt* the presence of that Kingdom; you understand that no words can explain it. The question, perhaps, is as to why one doesn't spend all their time there, in heart and mind. The absurdity of doing one's 'own' thing despite the impossibility of this ever being the case. Man is stubborn in spite of perfection; lacking the patience of Grace, he succumbs to the deficit of matter.'

'How can one not be stubborn in this way?'

'Who is being stubborn? Who is it who refuses to open, who runs from it as a child from thunder? We need to have a word with ourselves, at all times, in all things. Who is it who doesn't *know* of the Words in their heart? To be angry, spiteful, full of hate, jealous...and on and on, it is clear in soul that to be this way is wrong, and yet this is only understood after the fact, during the fact - the pull and draw of the Good is ever-present, it is only in our choice to look *away* that we fall for ignorance and evil.'

'And so how does one avoid doing this?'

'Young man, let us say you are in a river, the water is crystal clear, and yet you are unable to see the bottom. Protruding from the banks on both sides are all kinds of branches, clumps of grass, rocks and even overhanging trees, you can choose to grab onto these if you so wish. Sometimes this river is calm, sometimes it's even still, but other times it is rough, turbulent. As time continues, so too does this river, one of the most obvious flaws of man's own perception is that he believes someday, via his own actions, the river will just cease; in a certain way it *does* stop, but in other ways which are more important, one must understand that the river truly never halts.

What all men wish to do is anathema to Being itself, they wish to grasp and grab for fear of life at all which protrudes from the banks; identified with self-alone they thrash from side to side, cradling support after support; even the calmest are ignorant of the trickle of blades they quietly clutch in times of sorrow.

There comes a point in the river, where even a firm two-handed hold on a sturdy branch is nothing against the awe of the torrent; fear, respect, reverence and acceptance, collapsing into a loving-obedience. It takes time, and many will still touch upon a support to check they are still there, but at this juncture all men have but two options left.

First is true acceptance, blissful, carried away with Grace as grammar - I shall speak more on this in a second. For the second option is...strange. For these men know all is not equal, and they cannot *win* in the manner they seek to define it. They have come to understand that moth and rust shall destroy all supports, they *know* this. And yet, this is covered with a thick ignorance; their journeys become exercises in absurdity. When I state 'they know', I mean it is within them to be able *to know*, it is *of* them to know Truth, and yet they expend all in avoidance of what is ever-encroaching upon them. *They tell themselves in knowing that they know not.* It is a loop which only the heart can overcome. The peculiar fact here is this - the men of the second option believe others are within a different river, that their suffering, success, and fear is somehow different, that others have cooked some deal or have been given something they weren't. But no - everyone is equal in their approach along this river; but the relationship with it is everything, for one can transform misery into mystery, sorrow into purposeful suffering, ignorance into openness, and arrogance into acceptance. One must lean into the river with their Being; the world is not for *you*, it simply *is.* '

They sat for some time, the light of the barn retaining its glow, fluctuating a remembrance.

'So, *to see,* is to see no-thing, but also all things from the sight of He?'

'There is a great difference between what it is *to* see, and *seeing.*'

'Openness?'

'One can be open to many things, but in Truth only truly open themselves to One.'

'And that is...who or what, exactly?'

'It is true that I am a Messenger, but for such a question, there is no answer made of words which could suffice. You ask me the impossible, for you ask me of yourself.'

'Only for me?'

'Only for you. In this way, only you know, only you understand. No one can take this from you, nor even touch it; but all others who also see can share in some sense.'

'I see.'

'What gentle hope. And now we must go, the time here is up, and there are things still to be done.'

'Will I see you again?'

'Young man, you already know the answer. Farewell, you are doing so well.'

Barn faded, and the young man found himself before his familiar checkout.

~

And so I stood in my usual position, a hue evolving throughout. Entering from the main entrance, an everyday man, and yet unique in soul, a man, going about his day. Sonder, they say, is to look upon another and understand them in the sense that they too have the same rich inner-life as yourself, their own dreams, hopes and fears, their own family and friends. To look upon another, can be a removal of division. He shopped with calmness, and so arrived at the checkout.

'Just these please, and how are you?'

'Yes, I'm quite content today, yourself?'

'Oh, much the same!'

And off he went with a smile to warm his trace. A seemingly polite nothing, needless pleasantries reveal their need; the sincerity of a single party allows for something more; a momentary companion within life. Warmth found forever in the in-between, everyday rapture floating within. The slightest of actions and agency in communion with that Someone, the unspoken Word between all; only the silent hear, and to listen with a still intent is to revere the most delicate of choirs.

~

These days continue on, becoming clearer as they do. The fog of judgment lifting, allowing all free to exist in the merit afforded it. Everyone passed through, encapsulated in but a few, an assemblage of all men glorifying the best and worst of that which is to come, taken not as burden, but simply as it is. And you try and hold, attempt to grasp at all times - man loves to *try to adhere*, but the *attempt* is mere subjective adhesion, it is in openness that the objective comes forth. For what of kindness can accept the lure of material lifeboats; to grasp is to believe one can truly *acquire*, as if one doesn't have all they need within them already; there is no eternal acquisition except that which one had all along - and so what of all this non-sense of vanity, pride, the tables and chairs, the 'mine' of all in earshot - to lapse is to believe one *has!* When given over to others, and to the tranquility and patience, what can life offer but a chance *to offer?*

After one has taken all one can take, which is, in Truth, at the end of time, nothing but that which has already been given as granted, then what is left but only to give? If one's life is about self then life disappears, and all Grace targeted towards the outside is mutated and flipped inwards, as if one can become without any help whatsoever. To turn sight inward is to become blind in the depths of a self-created misery; to place oneself on a pedestal of one's own creation, and to look down upon all thereby deemed unworthy of such a position - in such moments of pride, I only listens to I; the question, then, what is it to listen without any self at all, to simply listen?

No more of self opinion, of what one believes others should say of self; step into the place of another, breaching the tyrannical cage of me, me, me, into the trepidation of a common vulnerability. Stepping into the open-open, all sides unbordered, without potential to *hold* something of one's own. Struck by a terror, a fear amidst such an expanse, but a fear of what? To take such a step is to accept an Above, able to offer what has been allowed to grow in head, heart and body; listen to the silent Word which arrives without language, have you anything to share of which you can give over without thought of self?

~

The store is, ultimately, a strange place. Not hostile, nor defensive, a no-man's land of the choice between hope and despair; and a single choice rang out higher than all others, to choose hope even in spite of assured defeat, what of hope then?

After my long discussion in the barn I was given more freedom - where I could go in the store, what work I could do, very little was off limits, if anything at all. Except that is, for discussion. At times I tried to get the attention of the other staff, full of various questions, to no avail. I was not ignored, nor shrugged off, but in time those questions which seemed a priority in a single moment, drifted into their Just box, more often than not, their enormous nature soon deflated; in time, silence answers all such questions.

~

Noise was lacking here, it was intermittent, noticeable and yet avoidable; perhaps a pure Rest is one in which all lines of enquiry are allowed a simultaneous singular reign, a place where distraction is impossible. There is not a sentence which can be tacked to silence as an improvement, for in Truth, within the attention of silence, one is alone with the Word.

~

I hadn't heard from my Messengers in a long time, but I intuited that all was well, and in moments of doubt, internal winds could be drawn into a fury, bringing forth a remembrance of a Home never visited; and soon enough, there was no need to *remember* at all.

~

It was an evening and I had been called to work on the shelves, the store quiet and empty. I found myself working adjacent to the back hallway. Whilst getting on with my task at hand she passed-by, acknowledging me, yet carrying on into the hallway without a word. As she passed I was lit up. I continued to work, and as I did, talk began to arise from around me.

'...And so what *shall* we do?'

'I know what you speak of, and we all have asked such questions since our arrival. Impatience is of little help.'

'It is an impatience in the face of increasing tension - things are getting far worse, are they not?'

'I am not so sure, as the shrill coldness infects further, so too does greater warmth triumph.'

'Such difficulty in seeing light in this ever-encroaching darkness.'

'It was always going to be difficult. And yet one must remember, that despite the clear contrasting designations of light and dark, white and black, Good and evil, that one 'side' has an end, and therefore, there has never even been two sides. Only the eternally triumphant against the forever ignorant. One can choose a side in a moment, allowing *occasions* to lead them away from the Kingdom, but such acts do not deny the Kingdom in its entirety, and are never truly able to.'

'These duties of ours, here and now, are they to end?'

'At the end of all days. Until then we are simply to continue, even if one is certain of defeat - especially in such cases.'

'Some look at the world and see very little worth looking at.'

'Of that which one sees, it is of no surprise that the worst-of-the-worst should appear forthwith, for the most detestable and lost are more often than not the loudest too. The content, the meek, the humble, these people have no need to scream, for they have no need to *display*. The Truth, quite ironically, is that which can be proclaimed only quietly, by those who have the patience for it. For it is a rare few who question why someone should need to proclaim *their* truth so loudly. For if it is in fact the Truth, as they say it is, why do these people feel such a need to yell and yell, as if in a state of panic? It is, arguably, an unfortunate aspect of Truth that it is delicate, reserved and even quite timid, it has no need to *declare* itself for it already *Is*.'

'And so we are just to carry on?'

'If man can still be led astray, then our work is not yet done. But we must never overstep our bounds.'

'It is a question of faith.'

'Such bounds are of their creation, and this is true for the bounds they create between themselves and those such as Ollneek. Belief in such borders quickly forms a mutated reality, for them, that is.'

'And to remove all barriers, speak with them directly, this is out of the question?'

'Men like to speak of a certain lesson I have become quite fond of, 'One can lead a horse to water, but one cannot make it drink'. It is much the same with ourselves and them; beauty and light cannot be coerced, for then their acts are done from a place which is inherently-material, as opposed to from a place of genuine Love.'

'I wish only that I could help more.'

'You help as much as you can. One could place a thousand obvious signs before the oblivious, and they would amount to nothing but further noise. Ollneek has developed many tricks in his days below, but the greatest of them all are those which distract man from himself, those which create an illusory idea of self for him to focus on and identify with. From here, man chases only an *idea* of what he could be, and such an idea is always stripped of the Divine. We can offer only what they *need*, and never what they want. If they aren't to look for us, or even to accept that such looking is the Truth, then we shall never be found.'

'Perhaps I am beginning to understand what men mean by being tired...'

'In recent years, I can most definitely sympathize. Now, I had been meaning to talk to you anyway. This young man, you have been with him quite some time recently, how are things?'

'He won't need to stay much longer, a little more and we shall disappear.'

'And you believe he is ready?'

'You know as well as I, it is not a matter of my own belief, if it is time for us to leave, then we shall leave.'

'Very well. And your thoughts on him?'

'He will do just fine.'

'When you know it is time, tell him what he needs to know.'

'I will.'

~

Some more time passed, the store often busy, the shelves filled with all kinds of vibrant coloured goods, the low hum of pleasant music occasionally breaking through from above. All kinds of custom. As I walked throughout the store on this day, I noticed the outside, the town via windows which had slipped past my vision before now. So much I had never seen, never sensed; life entered through all passageways long since forgotten. The town appeared almost whole, its material reality shining from behind, a passive splendor; intuition sung that there was to be more, and yet I understood there was no rush. Simplicity hung above all, no such complexities to overcomplicate morning birdsong or evening Autumn rain.

In time I came to understand that which you do not want to see, that which you wish to ignore, is surprisingly not the worst of yourself. For as one wishes *not* to look at such things, they admit to them within the very same act of reasoning. That which one actively avoids is only ever the eventual embrace of a forgiveness in waiting. Darkness as it is often propounded by doomsayers and cynics alike, is not in-itself a *part*, only ever a superfluous addition, a muddying of harmony.

I wished not to have to accept such forgiveness, not because to do so is to accept one was wrong, cruel or malevolent, for that is evident from the questioning itself. I wished not to turn my head in That direction for doing so would be to immanently create a regret already forgiven. The regret of being lost to He who was there all along, and upon such perception and acceptance, to be forgiven at once. And so my wish not to turn fully in That direction is because quite simply...I cannot fathom such mercy.

~

Time passed, the store was attended to patiently, and I took up work where I understood it was needed. I did all things as I did single things, with attempted shared resonance of that Voice which penetrates if you only allow it. In trying not to identify myself with my efforts, my successes and failures, I was often caught in a loop; pride enjoys chasing its own tail, and will do so all day if one doesn't cease their chatter. Of my thoughts now, even when greeted with unceasing limitrophes of despair, hope presides as a patient King; suffering at the hands of a modern malaise, where values fall away as rags from an old patchwork - hope and joy are found before all things, seated in-between all virtuous acts, hope is the grammar of the Good, and thus acts as the foundation of all Truth.

From the end of the aisle, she locked upon the young man, settling his being to a state of calm.

'Young man, you are still here. Still working.'

'Should I be somewhere else?'

'That is not up to me, but do you think you should?'

'I too am not sure, how could I ever know?'

'You already know. You know there is more for you than all this.'

'Why now?'

'You are standing with your head and heart above your feet. Try to keep it that way the best you can.'

'And so what now, will I need to see the others?'

'I am the only one here now. I can always hear you, but not always from here.'

And with this all but the young man and the Messenger disappeared, leaving a rural path at his feet.

'This is a path back to town, the gate at the end is often stiff. I believe you are afraid of one final task. For now, I must leave you.'

'Thank you.'

And with that she was gone.

PART 3: A SHORT WALK

She was correct, throughout the strings of all emotion remained a few knots, overlaps and crisscrosses of tension, relics of material confusion. But surely, I could not, could I? Such simplicity is anathema to modernity in spirit; the weight to accept that so small of a thing could dissipate all locks, heal all voices which call out. Before me a light brown path, a few stones, grass banks on either side, the blades of grass arching into their given light. Trees hang overhead to retain the warmth of journey, air shifting to the only rhythm, clouds glowing fragile against a sky washed blue; the rustling of a gentle breeze, the tip-toeing of birdsong as structure of Joy - and, cascading from within an openness found, eternal warmth seeking its source; for an infinite few seconds existence trembles as perfection revealed...

'Lord Jesus Christ, son of the living God, have mercy on me, a sinner.'

...a decade within a moment, and a rise of tranquility, the vertical arose amidst the plain as the path settled to a support. I halt before all that is, embracing it as is. Air within and without combined, sound at ease, and reality at eye-level, movement ceases...I can finally step. The most minor taste of Rest abound within that first sigh of heart; at once and eternally, one continues if only for hope of He, of God.

~

I walked to the end of the pathway, the gate swinging open freely. It opened into the town. In front of me is that which not so long ago was behind thick glass, within sight, but bereft of connection. No one notices me, though I am not ignored; all quiet, all went about their business in an orderly, yet distinct manner. The buildings, once but lines in the sky, now filled with content, lives blossomed and everyone was complete with history. To look upon someone, to delve into a tragic individuality; hope, despair, might and Love, leading into a stream of men united.

The town center is a polite bustle, I turn to where the store would have once stood, all I saw was a small dated building, inside were normal workers. One of them caught my eye, gave me a downwards nod, and quickly looked away, not recognizing me. Nothing resonated as I scanned the building, and all here was fine, but it was not for me. I looked around a while, and carried on.

~

And so I think, arising from such waters, of home, and so I think no more, and head in the direction of heart, where home seems to be. A location not of space, but of memory. Before me now an old street, small, with brickwork which shall one day cease. Houses leaning slightly, wooden frames, and internal chatter; flower boxes draped, all was soft. After four terrace houses, a left-hand turn. I kept close to the wall, all holding together without effort, all attentive of all. The lane declined and even the shadows held back, a sweetness taking precedence in sight. Halfway down, to my right, more homes, small wooden windows looked into the lives of many, potentials of personal familial flight. Pockets of life disconnected by material alone. Families, couples, singles, all resonating a Being given as granted, and not taken as such. In their actions, their very lives, a journey of recovery is undertaken, each window a beacon into the Goodness of hearts, each agency a signal unto itself up to the Above. The end of the road was tight, I have no clue as to how people get down here, a little overgrown with the foliage dragging against my sides.

A right-hand bend with high fencing along it - I know, I am here. A few steps further and I understand home awaits me - what to do but walk? And so I walk. Before me...nothing. Not a void, but an expanse of grass where a memory had been. I am not disappointed, the grass itself was a nice sight. But then the question of where to go, what to do?

~

To walk, to continue, but to where? All choices were split in two, of here, or of the Kingdom. The choices of here were infinite and yet amounted to nothing, the choice of the Kingdom was solitary, and yet eternal; there was only one choice then, and one ignorance; misery or hope? I shall go where I shall go, which is with my feet.

What I had learnt of decision, the only one which matters is the one most often accepted after all others, which should have come first. I hadn't anything to prove, no one to see, nor anything I wanted - elsewhere, in another time or place, I would have been lost, deemed depressed, but here, in the forever-now, all except the guiding warmth of Love fell away.

~

At times walking seems slow, life lived unto a pace declared by my attention alone, and so it passed into memory as gently as it arose. To return the way I had come, I had seen what I needed to. Back off up the path from which I had arrived, beginning to think of many things; the future, other vocations, exercise, self-care, possibly even a wife and children, I became almost dizzy with such thoughts. My feet followed the pace of my mind and before I knew it I was at the top of the hill. Turning the corner, muttering to myself of my future to come. My mental murmurs and wishes carrying me, I continue along the road, before me now my point of departure, this area too, now, simply grass. I turned to where I thought the store might be, also, just grass.

Now it is overcast and quite dreary. And so I try to look upon passing trees as I once had, but they do not hold, and yet I do not stop. I was now a little damp, a little heavy. Some time at a forgotten bus stop, in front of it is what seemed to be the remnants of a road since forgotten. A place only of temporary waiting. The sky continued lashing at the earth, and in the distance a few crashes rang out, such sounds disturbing nostalgia itself. The grass grew, cities fell, time itself left me alone, a confusion drifted over the horizon.

Drifting just above the tree line a dark sponge came forth, spanning the entire horizon-line. None of this made sense to me, and yet I know I have to continue. I can bring myself to say God, but to approach Him, to ask of Him...

As I dwell on this thought, of apprehension before the Lord, the hue of darkness grew closer, all places of rest ceased within what surrounds, and I am alone with choice of heart. The black shape folded into definition, before me a woodland, thick and gnawed. I am not able to see through to the other side, not a streak of light pierced this pitch, and yet, a pull and a push and a step of self, and suddenly I am within this forest.

Surrounding me, brazen and quietly arrogant, are a host of artificial oaks ascending to points; to look up is to look down, left and right, it is to look nowhere; but I have my compass. A wind shattered all stillness, confusion rained, and reality dampens itself. For weeks I have been walking with only heart for company; though, of course, I could have always simply stopped, but there I would have ceased altogether.

And so I leap between the protection of treetops against the rain, sitting under thin canopies for hours at a time. Soon enough, sitting allows no rest, and my feet ache only more;

whistling launched itself into a vacuum, and humming makes me nauseous; and worst, my sight cannot hold light except in the form of shadow, all was blurry once again. Aghast, washed out, and blitzed into loss itself, I cast all faculties, reason and appeasement to the Kingdom, casting myself over to Hope; the woods would be as it is, and I would be how I am, I continue thus by listening alone.

My body became light, head and heart signed a truce, opening to a restful ceasefire, the path before me was to be how it was to be, and no reason nor frustration could alter that - darkness prevailed within its own logic and the storm continued, but it did so under the resonation of an internal eternal, the Word echoed throughout all sense, and not an iota of Love was lost. Implicit within Glory is acceptance of intermittent defeat, and yet inherent is the sight of a victory forever celebrated.

Within this forest of a day, everything attuned to the battles fought in multitudes, the spark amidst insurmountable black, a snap of fire against infinite tar. Time folds itself into two forms of retreat - light-to-light, and dark-to-dark - and as the darkness retreats into itself it becomes pure-nihil, and as light retreats unto itself it shines only brighter, revealing the vacuity of darkness; nihil negates nihil by reliance on light for its very existence. The *only* choice, God or nothingness, and yet the Lord has already won!

And the sunlight returns through the trees, arriving when it always would, as I step now, the forest clears, the leaves brighten and spring has come. I find myself outside the forest, looking back upon it, it dissipates into grass. Before me, waiting, sits a stream.

~

I sit down, before the stream, the cool grass holding me. All is steady, lit from the inside with an inextinguishable serenity.

The young man had made it to the stream.

Yes, I took my time I suppose.

More than some, less than others.

And now?

Quite right, and now.

Was this all me? These decisions and steps?

No one else could have made them, help and deterrence are just that, for they are not acts in themselves; advice alone cannot make a decision.

And the store, the bakery?

They were there, you were there, and now you are here.

...and Ollneek?

Still around, and always will be.

What do I do about that?

Whatever it is you do when it matters, no need to dwell on darkness during the day.

And you?

I've been here this whole time.

Thank you.

I already have your thanks, for you are here.

Time for me to make my decision.

I think so, young man, don't you?

Any advice?

At times you will think to yourself that all this makes no sense, and at these times you must strive to realize that it matters not if it makes sense to you, but if it makes sense of you. Now, farewell young man.

~

I am entirely alone, and a little time has passed. I stand up, listening to the Silence, as I do so I step forward, and into the water.

Printed in Great Britain
by Amazon